Sent and Received

This Mourning's E-Mails, Packaged With Prayer

M I C H A E L   B R A N D T

WestBow
P R E S S
A DIVISION OF THOMAS NELSON

WestBow Press books may be ordered through booksellers or by contacting:

WestBow Press
A Division of Thomas Nelson
1663 Liberty Drive
Bloomington, IN 47403
www.westbowpress.com
1-(866) 928-1240

ISBN: 978-1-4497-7469-1 (sc)
ISBN: 978-1-4497-7468-4 (e)
ISBN: 978-1-4497-7470-7 (hc)

Library of Congress Control Number: 2012920964

Printed in the United States of America

WestBow Press rev. date: 11/30/2012

Preface

By Michael Brandt

I'm Mike Brandt. Thank you for picking up this book.

Sent and Received is a compilation of unedited emails I sent to our family and friends during my wife's battle with cancer. It also contains the reflections of our daughter Kayla. Our third daughter's poignant narratives provide background and a framework for better understanding our story. Jeannie's brother Jim, who helped edit the work, also adds a touching tribute. Publishing the book was a team effort. This book would not be possible without the help of a planning team. The team consisted of a huddle of skilled advisors that included consultant Melissa Dykstra, my dear friend Steve Jankord, my nephews Sam Goodhope and Greg Breukelman, Jeannie's brother, Pastor James Johnson, and Kayla, a talented writer and the third of our four daughters. We are also grateful to the advertising agency, Breukelman Kubista Group, based in Sioux Falls. We also appreciate the help of Ruth Gunderson, a Minneapolis writer and editor we consulted. Many other friends and partners helped us pray this book into existence. All proceeds will go to the Pastors Brandt Legacy of Faith Foundation to help fulfill the Great Commission of Jesus Christ.

My hope for those who read it is twofold. First, I hope that the Lord of Life would be glorified. Jesus is the Resurrection and the Life, and He victoriously delivered Jeannie from her body of death. Second, I hope that each reader will be enlightened and strengthened by the Holy Spirit to face the inevitable trials of life.

Our crisis began with surprising news during a routine surgery.

On January 21, 2005, the day before Jeannie's 58th birthday, my wife was scheduled to have her gallbladder removed. She had experienced pains in her abdomen for a month or two. We all thought it was a minor issue. Jeannie kept herself in great health. She was a disciplined woman of God in every respect, both physically and spiritually. Exercise, healthy eating habits, and annual physical checkups were the norm of her life. Jeannie kept her teeth so clean that once she wasn't even charged for a six-month dental hygienist appointment. Considering my dental habits, that would be the ultimate dental miracle. So for me, that gallbladder surgery was just a minor bump in the road of life.

However, we were soon to discover God had a more difficult journey planned. Soon after the surgery began, the surgeon asked to meet me in a consultation room. With a heavy heart, he asked me to sit down. "Pastor, I'm saddened to tell you," Dr. Thaemert, a trusted friend and member of our church family, told me. "We have some serious complications. I wasn't able to remove Jeannie's gallbladder. There are inoperable cancerous growths surrounding it."

From that moment, I knew Jeannie's situation was very grave. In the following days, we learned how extensively the cancer had spread. Over the next four months, our Good Shepherd, Jesus Christ, lovingly guided us through the valley of the shadow of death. His rod and staff gently prodded and tenderly gathered us along the path of life. Daily, the physical evidences of decay were unmistakable. Yet, the manifestation of eternal life shined through the shadows.

Many of you have been down this same pathway. Some of you are currently walking in similar shadows. Others of you will, sooner or later, enter this valley. Whatever your situation may be, I trust the truths of this book will effectively minister to you.

Jeannie died four months later, on May 22, 2005, the day before my 58th birthday. Since that day, many have asked what blessings came out of that crisis for us. At first, it was hard to sort out just one blessing. Of course, there were the blessings of God's Word, there were the special intimate conversations with Jeannie, the people praying, the cards and letters – they were all gifts from God's hand.

However, one blessing did come to the forefront.

It is best stated in Psalm 46 and Psalm 73. "God is our refuge and strength," says Psalm 46:1, "a very present help in trouble." In the same way, Psalm 73:28a states, "But as for me, the nearness of God is my good." God's presence was and is our greatest blessing. He was there before the trouble came, He never left us for a moment, and He has not failed to be with me and my four daughters since the day of Jeannie's glorious home going.

Romans 8:28 also declares, "And we know that God causes all things to work together for good to those who love God, to those who are called according to his purpose." It does not say *all* things are good, but all things will *work together for good* to those who *love* Him and are seeking to do His will. This is the blessing God has sent. Jesus is available to all who call upon Him. If you haven't done so, ask Him to forgive your sins. Tell Him you love Him. He is the blessing, who can be *received* by simple childlike faith. Ask Him to come into your heart. He will. He is present. He will never leave you or forsake you, no matter how dark the shadows become.

If I can be of help, simply email me at pastorbrandt@knowingthesavior. org.

—Pastor M.W. Brandt, August 2006,
Sioux Falls, South Dakota

Chapter One: Introduction

James L. Johnson

Michael and Jeannie Brandt began their journey together at a Bible school in Los Angeles, where they studied and met in the mid-1960s.

Jeannie was the smart blonde from Minnesota. Michael was the edgy pastor's son from South Dakota. They were two Midwestern students in a small Bible school of 150 students in California and after graduation, they both moved back home and began to write and occasionally date. They let their relationship grow over several-times a-week letters over the next three years. They connected out of a common passion for the Bible and out of an unusual gift to help people. They wrote letters and traded prayer requests and saw each other occasionally for more than three years. After Michael's unceasing letters ("I wrote her every day," he insists) and his regular question – "Jeannie, do you love me?" – they finally were married in 1969. Together they served as a ministry couple in four churches over 36 years.

The love story culminates with the emails you are about to read.

For almost four decades, Mike and Jeannie Brandt made a great ministry couple. Michael's boldness and Jeannie's tenderness fed off of each other as they served four growing congregations. Mike felt the call to be a pastor soon after he began college and quickly gained a reputation as an outstanding preacher and evangelist. Jeannie was a nurse who cared about people instinctively and earned a name as a lady of grace and compassion. She was also an outstanding musician. Her bell choirs gained smiles and plaudits from hundreds of listeners, and her sterling soprano voice could leave you dead in your tracks. Life as a pastor's wife seemed like the perfect place for a woman with an instinctive knack to meet pressing needs. She and Michael clung to their urgent desire, just as strong as music and Mike's sermons, to make disciples of Jesus Christ. His preaching brought conviction; her personality brought compassion. The combination of sin and grace made them a delight to know – and a success in building churches. They worked and served together for 36 years, planting and serving Lutheran churches in Washington, Wisconsin, Minnesota and South Dakota.

Their love story ended with cancer.

Jeannie Brandt was diagnosed with cancer at age 57 and died four months later in May 2005. Michael dealt with her passing by preaching and writing his way through the crisis. "I have to walk through it," Michael told me, during Jeannie's battle. "The Lord will take me through it." You can't ignore the pain, he told me. He cared for his wife and came to the office when he could. And to avoid having to answer the painful questions over and over, Michael sent out regular email notices – most of which became insightful essays about what it's like to suffer.

The email updates published in this book cover the final seventeen weeks of Jeannie's life and the following months of Michael's mourning and insights. The updates end with the one-year anniversary of Jeannie's death, where Michael visits the countryside grave of his long-time ministry partner.

The twenty-six emails became known as "Pastor Brandt's emails," but we chose to call this book "Sent and Received: This Mourning's Emails." Two simple words, Sent & Received, became our grief and our hope all in the same instant. They were the two words that always appeared in the corner of our personal computers as we read the emails. The letters were always delivered in the morning and we were mourning as we read them, anticipating the inevitable. When we saw that familiar white envelope in the *received* box of our email browsers, our hearts beat a little faster and we took a deep breath as we anticipated news *sent* from Michael about Jeannie.

Even when the emails contained sorrow, we desired that the envelope meant an update from Pastor Brandt. We still longed for the hope of his words – still yearned to experience the journey of Michael and Jeannie's love story. Michael's email list grew as people heard about Jeannie's cancer. We watched Jeannie die in seventeen weeks and learned how to suffer – and say goodbye – as we read the emails. But as we suffered, prayed and hoped, the emails helped us cope with the eventual loss. In reading them, we learned to trust God. We learned the realities about death and cancer. And we learned that God "sent" Jeannie to us as He sends all His prophets, ambassadors and people – for a time. And then God "receives" them back. Heaven is our hope. Living for Jesus Christ is our purpose. Like the emails published here, Jesus was sent to give us hope and life. And we need to receive Him.

What follows are the lessons and insights Michael shared with us as he sent Jeannie back to the Lord. The first of Michael's twenty-six emails is next. Kayla Brandt, Michael and Jeannie's third-born daughter, tells their story in between. We publish it in the hope that reading our mourning's emails can point you back to the Lord, who alone can give you comfort in your mourning.

From: Pastor Michael Brandt <pastorbrandt@knowingthesavior.org>
To: Family and Friends in Christ
Subject: Jeannie Update 1/22/05

January 22, 2005,

Dear Family in Christ,

Some of you are at a loss for words. I know you are not at a loss for words ... you're just praying them to the only One who can meet our needs!

As you have heard, Jeannie's surgery revealed a more serious issue with cancer. We had some concerns, but were somewhat relieved after her ultra sound came back with only gall stones showing. However, the cancer was well hidden and Dr. Thaemert (a member of our church family) recognized it immediately. Due to the location and spread of the cancer, he could not remove the gall bladder or the cancer. Doctor Thaemert was and is a tremendous blessing to us. Doctors often have difficult news to deliver and they need our prayer support too. As the incision heals, we will be prayerfully seeking an oncologist's counsel with respect to any possible treatment. Surgery is not an option.

Many of you have been in difficult situations of life. We know God is in control of our lives. We all live in a fallen world where the trials of life come on the just and the unjust. However, those who follow Jesus have a strength and comfort not known to the world. It comes in the form of a person, the Holy Spirit. Day by day, He enables us to find in Jesus, His grace and mercy. Through the Word, He gives us insight, comfort, and strength.

We desire that God would miraculously make Jeannie well. In the matchless Name of Jesus, we make our desire known to Him. God is able, for He is the Great Physician. In humble faith, we simply say with Jesus, "Father, Thy will be done." His will is always right and our ultimate desire is for Jehovah God to be glorified, whether by blessing or trial, by life or in death.

Because of His grace and mercy, we have peace even in our storm. Today, January 22nd, is Jeannie's 58th birthday and in that we rejoice. Yes, I did get her a present!

With the David in Psalm 31:14, 15a, Jeannie and I say, "But as for me, I trust in Thee, O Lord, I say, Thou art my God. My times are in Thy hands ..."

Thanks for your support and partnership in the Gospel of Jesus Christ.

Pastor B

Chapter Two: I Asked Her to Marry Me on the First Date...

Kayla Brandt

Mom was a beautiful blonde, even in curlers. That's what Dad found out when he crossed paths with Mom for the first time in 1965 at California Lutheran Bible School in Los Angeles. Mom was on the yearbook committee for the Bible school and was searching for just the right male student. Her assignment was to photograph a CLBS student studying for his classes.

"How about that good looking boy from South Dakota?" a friend suggested. Dad was chosen, arrived for his photo shoot, and came face to face with his future bride.

Her strawberry blonde hair was piled high in rollers. Nevertheless, Dad was awestruck. A few days later, one of Dad's classmates suggested he ask Mom if she needed a ride to a prayer meeting. The real purpose was for Dad to find out more about the pretty, sweet Christian from Minneapolis. Dad was always bold. His photo shoot gave him an in, and Dad mustered the courage.

"You want a ride to the prayer meeting?" he asked. It was as romantic as he could do at the time. "I had several other sweep-you-off-your-feet lines like that one," he told us in his characteristic self-effacing humor. "But I was smitten from the moment she got in the car. I asked her to marry me on that first date." Though Mom refused his proposal, to Dad's surprise, she agreed to go out with him again.

Under his cool demeanor, jet-black hair, and widow's peak were Dad's crystal-clear blue eyes. He had the look of a brand new believer. During his senior year of high school in 1965, Dad surrendered his life to Jesus Christ and decided to go to Bible school. Mom looked into those eyes and saw his heart. And it was there that she saw Jesus. And so their story began. Besotted, Dad would call her from the hallway pay phone at his apartment building so his roommates couldn't listen. But while Dad would venture down to the hallway to dial her number, his roommates would dial Mom's number and tie up the line. Dad was persistent and continued to pursue Mom. He would not relent. Over the next summer, he wrote Mom no fewer than six letters a week. Mom's path after Bible school took her to Northfield, Minnesota, to attend nursing school. Dad ventured to attend college at The University of South Dakota in Vermillion. Three hundred miles separated them, but love letters bridged the divide.

Years later, Dad shook his head as he recalled, "It wasn't until three years later that your Mom said she loved me." Earlier in life, Mom had made a commitment before God to tell no man, except her father, that she loved him until she knew the man was God's choice for her. "Praise God, I was that man," said Dad.

It was said by those who knew Mom that it only took one meeting with Jeannie to fall in love with her. She was genuine. She had a look that said she cared. Dad said Mom's love felt so good. We agreed. Oh, to be one of the ones Jeannie loved!

How did Dad know when Mom loved him? Dad told us he knew it the first time she signed a letter, "Your Jeannie." It became their unique and precious sign of affection to each other. Every card, note, and letter was signed with this sacred mark of proud ownership, "Your Michael," and, "Your Jeannie." Dad requested Mom's hand in marriage on a bench at the Sioux Falls, South Dakota, zoo outside of Leo the Lion's cage. He continued to write love letters. Mom and Dad were hundreds of miles apart at the beginning of their courtship, but through those letters they formed an intimate bond that would unite the two in marriage on April 5, 1969, after many letters were sent and received.

The following article was written by Dad for Abiding Savior Lutheran's monthly newsletter. Dad and Mom served together as pastor and wife at Abiding in Sioux Falls, South Dakota, from 1991 to 2005. This article was written prior to learning of Mom's terminal diagnosis.

"Thy Word is more desirable than gold, yes, than much fine gold; sweeter also than honey and the drippings of the honeycomb,"
Psalm 19:10

When I fell in love with Jeannie, it was head over heels. Yes, she was the head and I was the heel. She swept me off my feet. I was smitten!

Most of our courtship took place through the mail. We were attending the same Bible college in California for only a few months, when she graduated and went on to St. Olaf College in Northfield, Minnesota. I returned to the Bible college and began what my folks call a miracle. I started to write letters.

Previously, in two years of school, I had written my parents only two times, probably for money. Now, I found myself writing to Jeannie every day. Even more so, I found myself waiting for the mailman like a well–timed clock. Why the change? Didn't I care about my parents?

For you that have fallen in love, I don't think I need to explain, but for others an explanation may be necessary. There is no doubt I loved my parents. However, these are two different types of love. They cannot be fairly compared. Both are genuine. My love for my family is a matter of the heart. Love for Jeannie is a matter of heart and soul. Already, the miracle of God's making us one was taking place.

Her letters were like honey to me. I read and reread them. I even tried to read between the lines (not a good idea). I was in love. Even today, one of the best ways of conveying our love for each other is through the written word (guys take a hint). The cards we give each other and the personal notes we pen are deep expressions of our heart's love. We listen to them, as we read them. They speak of love, commitment, faithfulness, care, compassion, and passion. They are priceless

This same priceless communication is what God desires in His relationship with us. A love where heart and soul are impacted to the point we long to read His love letter to us, the Bible. Listening to His Word and hearing His heart deepens our affection, just like the Psalmist said. This is our goal during the 40 Days of Lent. As you listen to the New Testament on tape or CD for 28 minutes each day, I believe your love for Jesus will be ignited, some for the first time. For others, it will be a time of renewing and deepening your love for Him. In either case, His love letter will prove more desirable than gold and sweeter than honey. Listen and see!

Chapter Three: Jeannie's Jesus

Kayla Brandt

Mom claimed Jesus as her Savior when she was a little girl. She had loved Him for as long as she could remember. She never wavered from that faith.

She was raised in a Christian home in Minneapolis. There her doting parents, Lyell and Lois Johnson, raised their family of six in a growing suburban church and a sprawling neighborhood. The carpenter and nurse pointed her to Jesus and read the Bible and prayed with their children regularly, living out their faith openly. Their example set in motion a life of discipleship for a young woman who embraced the Savior from childhood.

At age fourteen, Mom dedicated her life to Christ. Her life verse was II Corinthians 5:14-15, "For the love of Christ controls us, because we are convinced that One has died for all; therefore all have died. And He died for all, that those who live might live no longer for themselves, but for Him who for their sake died and was raised." It was a moment of decision, Mom explained to us, and she became "sold out" for Jesus Christ. Like Paul taught in I Corinthians 5, Mom became "convinced" that Christ died and rose again, and she sought to "live for Him" who died and was raised. Mom hungered for the Word and this desire led her to enroll at Bible school in California.

Her schooling at CLBS involved two intense years of Bible study, providing her with a foundation on which to build her life. There Mom became rooted in her faith and equipped with the Word to guide her decisions. During her Bible school years, Mom claimed another verse that became a lifetime favorite, Jeremiah 15:16: "Thy words were found, and I ate them, and Thy Word became to me a joy and the delight of my heart."

As her daughter, I saw up close how much of a delight the Bible was to my mother. My sisters and I recall the vivid image of Mom sitting in her rocking chair in the early morning hours having her quiet time with God. Her family still sleeping and the house silent, she would sit in the living room, her Bible resting on her lap as she nestled into the Word of God. There she prayed for her girls and many others whom she knew were hurting. She was a faithful prayer warrior. She knew the power of prayer and had kept a prayer journal for years. It was organized by month, and in it contained the names and burdens of loved ones and strangers. She had prayed many through trials. And this was how she began every day, kneeling at the feet of God in devotion.

Mom embraced the role of pastor's wife with ease. Though it was a capacity she had never anticipated filling, she ministered without hesitation along with Dad to many in the churches they served. Their first call in 1972 took Mom and Dad to Elim Lutheran Church in Lake Stevens, Washington – a new church plant where Mom and Dad made many friends quickly.

Dad was a shepherd. He had been gifted with the ability to evangelize and deliver the message of salvation with persuasion. Soon the church grew from twenty people to an attendance of two hundred. Christ spoke the truth through Dad, and many souls came to salvation wherever he preached. Dad planted seeds in the hearts of people; Mom pulled weeds and watered. Mom was a gardener.

Gardening came naturally to my mom. She loved to grow things. Her window boxes and gardens were a sight to behold every spring as they spilled over with splashes of color in petunias, geraniums, pansies, and impatiens. I remember Mom's delicate hands covered with soil as she lugged her bucket and spade, her face just beaming when the calendar hit the day after Mother's Day – the day she felt she had permission to plant flowers. A few years back, Mom had cut a small sprig from her mother's clematis and she planted it outside her front door. She watched on with caution as the weak sprig began to sprout and grow. She cheered it on as it began to latch on to the lattice and climb the east side of the house. And now every spring we watch Grandma Lois's clematis bloom with deep purple buds. We cheer it on as Mom's leafy legacy sends us a reminder of the beauty Mom possessed and saw in God's creation. Mom gardened souls the same way. When people came to faith under Dad's preaching, Mom watered, weeded, and looked on with delight as souls took root and grew. She urged them on like only a true gardener can do. Her thumbs were green.

She was an excellent teacher and received many requests from churches in the Midwest to speak at women's retreats or special events. She doubted her presentation skills and put tremendous effort into her preparation. But even with floundering nerves, Mom would dive into the call. She was a visual learner and liked to provide object lessons. I remember watching her color charts and pictures on tag board that she would use when she spoke. She was not an artist, so she would draw these funny little stick people to help convey her message. And somehow those unpolished stick people with triangle dresses and curly hair became masterpieces when matched with Mom's heart and voice speaking about her Jesus.

And then there was the music. Mom was passionate about worship and praise. Her voice soared in sweet soprano sounds, especially when she sang of Jesus. She had always been a member of the church choir and considered it a privilege to bring the gift of song to the congregation. She helped lead the praise teams that brought worship through music at the start of Sunday morning services. Again, her preparation was intense as she wove together Scripture and song. Adding an electric guitar, bass, and drums to the praise team were, at first, a stretch for Mom, but soon she embraced the desire of the musicians and led blended talents eager to serve Christ.

But it was her bell choir that brought her the most joy. In the late 1970s, while our family was serving a church plant in Amery, Wisconsin, Mom heard a bell choir at a convention. She was hooked. From that year on, she was forever linked to hand bell worship and introduced them again when my dad took a call in 1987 to St. Paul's Lutheran in Cloquet,

Minnesota. After much passionate persuasion from Mom, hand bells chimed at Abiding Savior Free Lutheran in Sioux Falls, too.

The task was accomplished by borrowing a local church's hand bell set and convincing her four daughters to polish up their ringing skills to perform a lively and tricky piece for a full congregation one Sunday morning. Our hands were flying as we swapped, swung, shook, malletted, and rang bells two at a time in each hand. I'm not sure if it was the actual sound of the music or the humor and fascination in watching five determined women sweating while they crisscrossed hands, jangled bells, flipped music pages and still managed to play the right notes at the right time that convinced the congregation. The bells were a hit.

Soon a gleaming four-octave set of hand bells appeared at the church. Mom was excited and dove into directing her bell choir. But she was sneaky. As her ringers began to learn, she would increase the difficulty of the music we were playing. First she would distribute a new piece of music to her novice ringers and casually turn on her portable CD player for us to listen to the professional bell choir perform the piece we were about to learn. We would all look at her with wide eyes and mouths agape as we listened to the rapid runs and the reverberating rhythms of a thousand notes playing all at once. We'd wonder how in the world she thought we were going to be able to play that piece. But she'd stand before us smiling with her eyes closed, relishing in the sounds of bells chiming. "Isn't that fantastic? You guys are going to be so great!" We were convinced she was delusional about our skills. But she would break the piece apart into small chunks for us to practice. Soon, under Mom's guidance, we kept ringing better and bolder. We were proud to be Jeannie's ringers. She was proud of us. Bells filled her soul with delight.

Those bell choirs became a metaphor for Mom's faith in action. Whether she was making music, leading a Bible study, serving coffee in the kitchen, or playing with children in the nursery, Mom's gentle demeanor reached out in love. She had faith in people and could see their abilities even when they couldn't. Mom instilled hope. Many have shared how her compassionate and tender ways were instrumental to their own personal faith. Mom had no idea how many people she touched, and she would never take any credit. She was simply walking the walk. It wasn't hard to see Christ in Mom. Jesus was on her face. People were drawn to her. They wanted what she had. They wanted Jeannie's Jesus.

From: Pastor Michael Brandt <pastorbrandt@knowingthesavior.org>
To: Family and Friends in Christ
Subject: Jeannie Update 1/27/05

January 27, 2005,

Dear Family of God,

Job said, "... Shall we indeed accept good from God and not accept adversity?" ..." Job 2:10

Jeannie came home from the Surgical Center yesterday. She has much discomfort, but the new pain meds are helping. She received great care from the staff there and from the many expressions of love you all have given in prayer, flowers, and cards. Our girls and extended family have also gone beyond the call of duty. I can understand why, Jeannie is easy to love. Thank you for your kindness to both of us. I'm blessed to be included in the halo of her care.

God has blessed our church with humble, servant leaders. Jeannie asked the deacons to come according to James 5:13-16 to pray for her healing and anoint her in the name of the Lord. They came in faith and God blessed Jeannie and me. Now we wait in childlike faith for the certain work He is doing. We have no doubt concerning our loving Father's care.

Jeannie has been diagnosed with squamous cell cancer. It has entered her blood stream. Surgically and medically, it is not curable, however that does not limit God's healing power. From what our surgeon said, he saw its growth surrounding several organs (liver, gall bladder, some bowels). It is a cancer often found in people who have used tobacco products or alcohol. You know me, I asked Jeannie if she had been hiding anything from me. She gave me her 'look' and I tried to behave myself. As many of you have experienced, sometimes followup tests verify these observations or reveal a different story. God is Sovereign. He knows all things. He will give understanding according to His will. That gives us peace, because no one loves us more than Him. Both Jeannie and I want His image to be refined in us through the heat of this trial. As a Master Refiner, Who values us, He will carefully burn the dross away for His glory and our good.

Today, January 27th, Jeannie has her first visit with her oncologist, Dr. Tolentino, at the Avera Cancer Institute. We are looking forward to meeting him and his staff. Pray that we might be a witness of Christ to each of them. God does gift men and women with medical knowledge and skills. They can wonderfully treat us, but it is the Great Physician Who heals. We are confident of God's healing power. We are also confident that His will is best. Our one desire is for His glory. We are praising Him for Who He is and all of His goodness to us. Please join us in giving Him praise.

Jeannie and I thank God for Bill Mitchell's (Parish Worker/Lay-Pastor @ Abiding Savior) faithfulness in sending out e-mail prayer requests. I also thank my mother and the phone prayer warriors, as well as, the teams of intercessors at our church. It is comforting to know that many are fasting and praying on our behalf. Added to that are the countless prayer chains and praying individuals we will probably never meet. May their reward in Heaven be great. Prayer is a Holy Spirit work made possible through the name and merit of God the Father's most priceless gift, JESUS! We praise Him for the privilege of breathing His Name in heartfelt expressions of faith. Even when words fail us, the Holy Spirit intercedes with groaning too deep for words according to the perfect will of God (Romans 8:26, 27).

Finally, Jeannie and I are blessed to be so well known. Many are upholding us in prayer. As pastor and wife, we are often in the limelight. Please remember that there are many others, even more precious to God, who are not in the limelight, but are suffering with similar needs. Some of them are suffering more than anyone can imagine. We are asking Bill to again list others on our prayer list who continue to be in need of our prayer support. Sadly, we forget to remember them all, but they are never forgotten by God.

Resting in the Palm of His Hand,
Pastor B & Jeannie

Chapter Four: She Tucked The Tickets Away For Me...

Kayla Brandt

When you grow up with the example of faith Mom provided, you don't question from where it came. We just knew that Jesus had always been in her heart. Mom's own words from a written testimony encapsulate it best. "Jesus loves me," she wrote. "This I have known since infancy, and I have loved Him, too, for as long as I can remember. As a young teen, I became aware that this 'good little girl' could never be good enough to earn God's favor, nor to secure a place in Heaven. Repentantly and joyfully appropriating Christ's death for me, I became assured of the gift of salvation. It is my highest honor and most exciting pleasure to be a container for the life of Christ." We, her four daughters, witnessed Jesus in the container of Mom day in and day out.

For me there was a moment of distinction, however, when the natural normalcy of Mom's faith grew into something special. It was February 2004, the night before Mel Gibson's *The Passion of the Christ* was scheduled to open nationwide in theaters. A private viewing had been arranged for several of the pastors and church leaders in Sioux Falls. As a ministry couple, Mom and Dad obtained a handful of extra tickets. One of these tickets Mom tucked away for me. I was an avid movie-goer and Mom knew it was a perfect opportunity for my eyes to be opened to Christ.

Even though I was a pastor's kid, I had wandered far from the roots of faith Mom and Dad planted.

Sadly, I was not a follower of Christ, but God was working. The theater was hushed that night. The special showing of *The Passion* stirred an immoveable silence that fell upon the theater as our eyes watched the agonizing pain Jesus suffered when He went to the cross. I was sitting next to Mom and listened to her weep. She watched her Savior beaten, whipped, bludgeoned, pierced, and nailed on that cross. And I watched her. I was startled by the graphic depiction of Christ's suffering in the movie, but it was listening to my mom speak of it afterward that struck at the very core of me. Mom and Dad and another couple from church invited me to join them at a restaurant afterward to talk about the movie. None of us had an appetite after viewing Christ's tortures, but we lingered long at the table to talk about the film. One by one we vocalized our reactions. It was my mother's tears that made the movie real to me. She was broken. God staggered her. She was wholly overwhelmed by how Jesus suffered, how He was lashed, what He endured. "He did all of that for me," she whispered to us.

It was personal and real. It was just Mom and Jesus. Her heart ached with sorrow for the pain Christ endured. It was impossible to listen to her and not grasp the reality of the gift of salvation she experienced. Impossible to not realize the magnitude of the price paid for that gift. I remember looking at Mom differently after that time on. I could finally see the bond between her and Christ for myself. She had a connection with Jesus that I couldn't comprehend at the time, but I could not ignore.

I could not deny this connection to Jesus, either, as I watched what happened after she went in for a routine surgery to remove her gallbladder on January 21, 2005.

Mom and Dad prayed a simple prayer together, "Guide the doctor's hands as he removes Jeannie's gallbladder and bring healing to her body afterward," Dad prayed. But the prayers for healing had only just begun. Little did we know that when the surgeon would make the initial incision, he would immediately realize that something was terribly wrong.

From: Pastor Michael Brandt <pastorbrandt@knowingthesavior.org>
To: Family and Friends in Christ
Subject: Jeannie Update 2/2/05

February 2, 2005,

Dear Friends in Jesus Christ,

Like Habakkuk 3:17-18, *"Though ...(everything may seem to fail)..., yet I will exult in the Lord, I will rejoice in the God of my salvation. The Lord God is my strength, and He has made my feet like hinds' feet, and makes me walk on my high places."*

Since our last message (sorry it was so lengthy), Jeannie has met her oncologist (Dr. Tolentino, a wonderful believer in Christ), had a chest x-ray, nuclear bone scan, and a barium CAT scan, had a surgical procedure to implant a prot-a-cath, revisited her oncologist to review the tests and talk about possible treatments, scheduled another visit with her surgeon (Dr. Thaemert, a member of Abiding Savior and a believer in Christ) to setup a possible colonoscopy and endoscopy, while we wait for the abdominal surgery site to heal. From Thursday, January 27th to Tuesday, February 1st, it has been a whirlwind. However, our feet and our faith have not slipped. Praise be to God!

God has gifted our two doctors with skill and humility. They acknowledge that from the simplest to the most impossible cases, physicians treat, but only God brings healing. Both doctors are consulting with other physicians and medical facilities. If chemo treatments are undertaken, the surgery site needs to be sufficiently healed first. Knowing the primary source of the cancer would help the oncologist determine the best chemo recipe. Having time to do additional tests may help them determine the primary source of the cancer. Cancer has been observed throughout the liver, around the gall bladder and transverse colon, lungs, and a 'hot spot' (nuclear uptake) on her left shin.

Jeannie is on a new pain med. It is a patch. We believe it has caused some of her recent vomiting (not my cooking). The notes on side effects say it may take a few days for her body to adjust to the med. Many of you know about these adjustments. None of them are easy, even when the overall result is good. Jeannie has been a trooper. The oncologist believes some of her pain is coming from the surgery site, but even more from the cancer in the liver. Therefore, he wants to do the best he can with pain meds so no further damage would be done to the liver.

We have been reading a Max Lucado devotional guide to the 23rd Psalm each evening. What a blessing. Jesus, our Good Shepherd, is providing, leading, protecting, and blessing us. These 'shadowy' valleys, where fears and dreads come upon us, are daily being transformed into wonderfully enlightened experiences of His all encompassing presence. Please praise His blessed Name with us. We love Him and thank Him for loving us! We love you too!

Keep praying for as we do for you. By the way, thanks for all the cards and flowers. Caring for all those flowers is opening a whole new career opportunity for me.

Resting in Our Shepherd's Care,
Pastor B and Jeannie

Chapter Five: Cry Out to Jesus...

Kayla Brandt

The news knocked the wind out of me.

It was like breathing in a rush of cold air that left your body frozen and motionless for a moment too long. I frantically gasped for my next breath.

"Cancer?"

My voice choked the word in disbelief.

Dad's explanation echoed in my head. I had risen from my chair and was standing now at my desk at work, only hearing half of the words as everything around me started to spin. The words became a hollow echo. Dad could hear my vulnerability, my gasps for breath, my confusion, all the strength escaping the daughter who had been so strong and independent. With his third daughter broken, Dad stopped talking and began to pray. He pointed me to the only One who could cover me at that moment. I felt God's grace.

Shaken and rattled, I must have been vocalizing the questions that were rushing through my head. A co-worker standing next to me wrapped her hand around my waist, her other hand clutched my arm. The weight of the news buckled my knees.

"Where is it?" I said. "Did they remove her gallbladder? Has it spread? Have you called the other girls? I'll be right there."

It was not the conversation that was supposed to take place. Mom had gone into the Sioux Falls Surgical Center early that morning for a routine gallbladder removal. I had talked to my sister, Alisha, before leaving the office for lunch.

"Have you heard anything from Dad on how surgery went?"

She hadn't.

"I just tried to call Dad's cell phone for an update, but he didn't answer," I explained to Alisha. We both hesitated for a moment, but conceded that everything was certainly fine. In fact, "I'm sure they're home by now," I said.

I made a quick call to the house to see if they were indeed home already. My tendency to panic was quickly setting in, so I called directly to the surgical center and asked for the director of nurses in the recovery room. Mom, a registered nurse, worked at the surgical center and I had worked as a nurses' aide there a few years before. I knew that they would give me an update on Mom's recovery process. The voice on the other end of the line recognized who I was.

"How is my mom doing?" I asked.

Joni fumbled over her words. She replied that she would get my dad on the phone. I should have realized there was a yellow Post-it ® note with a "+" sign on Mom's chart. That was the method the staff in the operating room used to warn the staff in the recovery room that a biopsy or surgery had uncovered malignant cells. It was the indicator to proceed with extreme caution and tenderness when interacting with the patient and family. Post-it® notes had a way of ruining your day.

When Dad got on the phone, there was something about the slow, methodic tone of his words that moved me to expect the worst. It was as though he had memorized what he was going to say to us girls. He had sat alone for hours before telling anyone as he watched Mom sleep off the effects of the anesthetic. He had studied his beautiful bride while the reality of illness loomed in the sounds of beeping monitors, IV tubing and pumps. Sitting there, he collected his thoughts before mustering the strength to start making the phone calls that would spread the news. My call came before he was ready. Dad's request was that we gather together as a family. He asked his four daughters to come to the surgical center. He wanted us and knew that we needed to be together.

I remember the short drive from my office to the surgical center well. I begged God out loud, repeating the same five words, "Please don't take my mom ... Please don't take my mom ... Please don't take my Mom." I knew it was fruitless to make promises to do or not do this or that if He would just spare her. But that knowledge didn't stop me from pleading with the God whom I knew could do the impossible.

Erika, my oldest sister, was in the middle of Wal-Mart with her two toddlers, three-year-old Isabelle and two-year-old Wesley, when her cell phone rang. She had been searching for the right birthday card for Mom, whose birthday was the next day. Dad's words were simple. The doctor had found cancer. Erika dropped everything, scooped up her children from the cart and rushed to her vehicle. Her husband, Sherwin, was working and she couldn't reach him. Her mind raced as she pieced the story together. Mom hadn't been feeling well since November. It was now January. She had been experiencing unsettling stomach and digestion problems. A mysterious pain in her left shin. Losing weight too quickly and unintentionally. Now it all made sense.

"Why are you crying, Mom?" her little girl probed. Erika didn't even have a chance to respond before Isabelle intuitively filled in the blank. "Is it the owie in Gramma's stomach?"

Erika sat in wonder at her little daughter's grasp of the situation. Young Isabelle had been able to connect the dots between their bedtime prayers the night before and the tears that now fell.

Erika, the listener among my three sisters, absorbed Dad's methodical explanation. We stood in the hallway of the hospital just 100 feet away from Mom's room. Dad had spoken the information out loud several times, and it was starting to sink in. Erika's legs and gaze drifted to Mom's bed. She grasped Mom's hand and studied the mother we all loved. It was there that the weight of the news fell with Erika to her knees and she gasped in her next breath.

Alisha, the second eldest daughter, was at home when Dad's call came. It was an ordinary day for her, mid-afternoon and nearing the time for her to pick up her kids, nine-year-old Isaac and six-year-old Emma, from school. Dad had learned from my shock to take a softer and slower approach. He explained that surgery had revealed cancer, but said little more about the severity of the situation. Alisha was taken back, but not yet startled. Her urgency settled in when she called her husband, Darryl.

"I'll come right home from work," he told her.

Darryl's response moved Alisha into the next realm. It's just cancer, she thought. Cancer can be treated. Cancer can be removed. Lots of people get cancer. "But it's cancer… in my mom," she said. This cancer was personal and brought a wave of emptiness into her chest. The usual short drive into town became the longest drive of Alisha's life. She was scared, but didn't cry.

The sight of Mom lying pale and helpless in the hospital bed drew out all of Alisha's compassion. Alisha is filled with compassion. As her heart ached and spilled over, she knelt down next to Mom and grasped her hand. She finally cried. She had gotten to Mom.

Ona, the youngest of us four girls, had it the toughest. She was many miles away in Grand Forks, North Dakota, living with her husband, Ben, when her phone call came. Child-like and unassuming, Ona, a newly married bride with a strong sense of perception, can read people in an instant. It didn't take more than Dad's question, "Is Benjy with you?" to understand that what Dad was going to say couldn't be good news. The time and space between us and a January winter blizzard would prevent her from kneeling at the side of Mom's bed that day. But it didn't stop the urgent and heavy longing. Dad's voice echoed the fourth time to his youngest daughter the reality of the cancer. Dad passed the phone to Mom, still under the haze of pain medication and anesthesia. Mom's words comforted Ona like a hand bell choir. She hushed Ona's fears.

She did the same for me that afternoon. I remember sitting next to her, holding her hand, tears beginning to well up in my eyes.

"Don't be sad, Kayla," she said and smiled.

The tears pricked at my eyes, but I refused to let them spill. It wasn't until later that evening that I cried hard. I had gone to Mom and Dad's house to pick up some personal items for Mom. I thought that she would want her own things. Lotion that didn't smell like medicine, a little makeup, pretty pajamas instead of a hospital gown. Necessities. I rushed around the house, stuffing every stupid bathroom item I could think of into her travel bag. I was being ridiculous and irrational. I was in a hurry to get back to Mom, and knew that every single personal item I was packing was pointless, but I was desperate to do anything that might make her feel better.

I was heading down the stairs to the door when I remembered. "She'll want her bathrobe."

I spun around and climbed the stairs two at a time. It was hanging in its usual spot behind the bathroom door. My hand reached out to grab it, the softness of the velour and cotton mix brushing against my skin. I pulled it down from the hook and drew it toward my face. I breathed in the soft, sweet smell of my mother, and my world came crumbling down into that wad of cotton cloth. It extracted every ounce of sadness in me. Every last tear that had been mounting inside of me that afternoon poured out into that ugly, worn, tattered purple robe. I sat there on the toilet and sobbed into my mother's bathrobe.

We all cried hard that night. As I cried, I remembered a phrase my mother would use frequently when comforting me. She had used it with all of us, "Cry out to Jesus." We knew that we were not ready for what was about to come, and so we gasped in those cold breaths of air and settled into the journey God was about to take us on as a family. That very night we began what would become a routine for us over the next weeks – we cried hard, alone, and in the privacy of our homes so that Mom would not see how sad we were. We wept. We cried out to Jesus just as though we were singing a song. It was a song to which we didn't know the words or tune. But it is what Mom had told us to do, anyway. "Cry out to Jesus." She had said it to all of her girls. And we were crying.

From: Pastor Michael Brandt <pastorbrandt@knowingthesavior.org>
To: Family and Friends in Christ
Subject: Jeannie Update 2/9/05

February 9, 2005,

Dear Family,

"And the Lord is the One who goes ahead of you; He will be with you. He will not fail you or forsake you. Do not fear or be dismayed," Deuteronomy 31:8.

This was a great word given to Joshua through Moses from God. It was good enough for him and it is good enough for Jeannie and me! Praise God for the witness of His faithfulness recorded in the Bible. We know He is the same God today. He does not change and He does not lie. Praise be to His holy Name!

The result of Monday's tests came back. All the biopsies were negative (PTL). Jeannie's visit yesterday was to her gynecologist. He too said everything he examined was clear. Though we want to know where the primary source of this cancer is, we are also thankful to know where the cancer isn't!

Jeannie's oncologist called and said we would begin chemo next week. His nurse will set up the appointment with us (no call yet). We will let you know so you can continue to pray. It makes us nervous to think about the treatments and their side-effects, but Christ is going ahead of us. He is already in the days ahead, preparing the way for everything Jeannie will go through. Therefore, His presence now drives the fears away.

We hope your prayer life is being enriched. Not only praying for us, but finding yourself interceding for many and communing with Jesus in a refreshing and deeper way. Jeannie and I are experiencing this blessing. Today we begin our 28 minute a day listening to the New Testament on CD. By Palm Sunday, we will have listened to the entire New Testament. "Faith comes from hearing and hearing by the Word of Christ," Romans 10:17. There is no better way to strengthen our faith.

Maybe you could pray for an increase in appetite for her and a lessening for me. She needs to be built up for the rigors ahead and I need to look better. Jeannie also said I need to avoid a heart attack, so I can take good care of her. Wow, what compassion she has!

Jeannie has received so many encouraging cards and letters. She has also been the recipient of many great spiritual books and CDs of Godly music. Thank you for your kindness to us. I told her I knew she was going to live here on earth a long time, because it will take forever just to read and listen to all of them!

Feel free to pass this word along to anyone who would pray for us or anyone you feel it would benefit from our journey of faith in Christ.

By The Grace He Gives We're Following Jesus One Step At A Time, (He knows where we're going!)

Jeannie and Michael

Chapter Six: Hope for the Hurting...

Kayla Brandt

My dad's emails began the next morning. By the time Mom's cancer was diagnosed, they had been serving Christ through pastoral ministry for more than 30 years. After all those years, my parents had accumulated quite an extended spiritual family. Mom and Dad's ministry at Abiding Savior Free Lutheran had begun with a group of thirty to fifty believers and had grown in fourteen years to more than 1,500 members and friends by the time of Mom's diagnosis. God had blessed the church beyond measure and continued to do so as my mother faced an impending battle with cancer.

Dad's regular emails served as a means to communicate the news and progress of Mom's illness. We knew that there were many who would lift Mom and our family up to God in prayer. Through the emails we asked that other believers would join us in praying for a miracle of healing. Many were already praying for her, knowing that she was scheduled for a surgical procedure. They adored her and loved her. It was hard not to. Mom was surrendered to Christ and the Lord radiated through her. Every touch of her hand and word from her mouth bore testimony of her walk with Jesus. She was a child of God, unashamedly and openly, and through her uninhibited faith others were brought to the saving grace of the cross. She abandoned this world. She rejoiced always. She prayed without ceasing.

The emails allowed us to learn the lessons with them. Mom and Dad embraced the trial. They did not flinch. They knew, allowed, and accepted that God was in control of their lives. They were assured through the truth of His Word that there was no better place to be than in His perfect will. Mom and Dad clung to each other and Christ. This unity to Christ and each other exemplified Ecclesiastes 4:12, "A cord of three strands is not quickly torn apart." This cord of three strands – Mom, Dad, and Jesus – became thicker, tighter, and stronger. We saw that in Dad's letters. They held on to each other as husband and wife, and Christ held them in His protective hand.

One of the first signs of God's grace and control was exhibited without doubt that Sunday. It was a heavy day. People were shocked. They were at a loss for words. But God's perfect timing and perfect will was confirmed, and the events of that weekend bore evidence of His sovereign control.

God provided the first measure of strength months before when Dawson McAllister, a nationally respected youth speaker, was invited to preach at our church that Sunday.

Initially, Dawson had turned down the request, but members in our church were persistent and asked again. Dawson later conveyed that he had wrestled with the request. Sioux Falls, South Dakota? What in the world was going on in Sioux Falls, and why would God want him to go there? Dawson later told us that he takes a break only two Sundays each year. His national radio ministry requires him to broadcast live on Sunday nights. One of the Sundays he devotes to time with his family; the other Sunday is reserved for a speaking engagement. In 2005, the speaking engagement brought him to Abiding Savior. He didn't know why he was coming, but God was tugging at his heart, a tug that he couldn't ignore. He heard and answered God's call.

As the speaker that Sunday, McAllister was one of the first to be told of Mom's illness. Dad had called him that Saturday afternoon to apologize for not being able to attend the youth event that night. He needed to be with his wife. McAllister understood and covered Dad with a meaningful prayer. That was when he realized why God had brought him to Sioux Falls. What was there? A hurting minister and his wife, a broken congregation, and a pulpit to fill that Sunday. McAllister spoke at all three services that Sunday morning. Though he barely knew our mother and father, he loved them in Christ. He was broken himself at the tremendous sadness of our burden. By God's perfect grace he was given the right words at the precise moment to share with the congregation. We girls attended church together that Sunday. We sat huddled in the pew with our Kleenexes in hand, clinging to each other. The youth speaker brought healing to our whole family that Sunday – to the congregation, the daughters, and to Mom and Dad especially. Even a skeptic could not ignore God's hand in it all. His mercy and grace was already sweeping over us.

Following that weekend, Dad's emails became a salve during our mourning.

They were sent to family, friends, and the congregation. In turn those letters were forwarded to other friends, connections, coworkers and neighbors. They spread like wild fire across the city, across the Midwest, the nation, and to other countries across the globe.

The neighbor across the street from Mom and Dad learned of Mom's illness when he was forwarded an email by a co-worker. South Dakota's Senator John Thune received the emails from a friend who received them. Brothers and sisters in Christ in the Czech Republic, Mexico, Rwanda, and many other countries received the emails and lifted us up in prayer and sent responses back. A compassionate doctor many states away, a man we never met, offered to pay all expenses incurred if we desired to send Mom to other hospitals, research clinics, or cancer treatment facilities. A local church called to ask for permission to use the emails as their study materials in a husband-and-wife Bible study group. We were flooded with people wanting to extend help in any way that we needed, whether it was food, work, money, or prayer. People were willing to do anything. Our family was astounded by the response.

My sisters and I were approached at the gas station and grocery store by strangers who recognized us as Pastor Brandt and Jeannie's daughters. They asked us, "How do I get on that email list?" We would try to explain that it wasn't really "a list," it was just messages being sent from our Dad about our Mom. We would instruct them to call the church and request that their name be added. People were hurting. They were facing their own unique and individual trials. They were hungry for the truth, for hope. And so the emails began to bring hope to the hungry and hurting.

Mom and Dad willingly allowed others in on the details of their personal and intimate journey. Their hope was that God would use their trial to bring others to Christ. What began as an effort to effectively communicate to as many people in one sitting as possible grew to become an extension of Mom and Dad's ministry. No longer were the emails simply a report on Mom's condition; the gospel was being spread. God was using Mom's trial and Dad's words to bring Him glory. Mom and Dad were God's vessels by setting an example of a marriage in Christ, the strength that God delivers His children in times of trial, the mercy God gives when we allow Him to hold us, and the grace that He grants even in death. The emails began to be sent and received.

From: Jeannie Brandt
To: Family and Friends in Christ
Subject: Jeannie Update 2/14/05

February 14, 2005,

I want to thank you for your outpouring of love the last three weeks, but words cannot express what I truly feel. Would you look beyond my tear–filled eyes to the deep places of my heart and understand how grateful I am? I love my Abiding Savior/Living Word family. I am blessed to have you surround me at this time.

Thank you for your cards, bookmarks, artwork, flowers, food, bathrobes, CD's and devotionals. I humbly receive them all, and love you for your thoughtfulness. The quilt is an amazing gift—a "touchable" blanket of your presence with me daily. Most of all (and I do mean "MOST"), I thank you for praying for me. It is the most powerful thing you can do for me, and I sense the hand of God moving in response to your prayers. Keep telling me what your children say…their faith is powerful and comforting.

You may know that I am having trouble eating well since surgery. Michael and my daughters thoughtfully dish up my plate every day, and I am trying to eat up what they serve me. This picture is very much like the way I visualize the Lord's hand in my life. You see, I have loved Jesus for as long as I can remember. He is my Savior, my Shepherd, my Friend. . . He is my All in

All. From the time I was born, like a loving parent, Jesus has been dishing up my plate of life. He has been so good to me, spooning up just what I've needed— great, tasty food that has nourished me and helped me grow. I have feasted on His delicious cuisine. Occasionally he has dished up some items that have looked questionable to me. I haven't even wanted to try them, but when I finally swallowed them, I've discovered His choice has been best for me, giving me extra strength that I could not get from any other food. Sometimes He has dished up spoonfuls that were not pleasant at all, and even when I thought I had finished, He would give me a little break and dish up the same thing again! Even this food I have learned is "just what I needed" for endurance and character. Now He has dished up something really big. I am trying to poke my fork in it and taste it, but the first few bites have been kind of hard to swallow. I know He has never disappointed me. All the items He has put on my plate have been needful and GOOD. So I will chew away, and by His grace, finish the course. Please pray that my appetite will improve, literally and spiritually!

"In Thy book they were all written, the days that were ordained for me, when as yet there was not one of them. How precious also are Thy thoughts to me, O God!"

Psalm 139:16, 17.

With deep affection,
Jeannie

Chapter Seven: Accepting the Diagnosis...

Kayla Brandt

The two and one-half weeks that followed Mom's diagnosis were chaos.

We were overwhelmed with dozens of tests, appointments, lab draws, consultations, x-rays, CAT scans, bone scans. The lists went on and on.

Mom's poor body was poked, pricked and prodded to no end. She trooped through with unfaltering courage. She would not complain. We knew by then that her diagnosis was terminal. The intent was to buy more time. The purpose of the tests was a maddening search for the primary source of this infrequently seen cancer. Mom's healthy lifestyle should not have made her prone to such a disease. Doctors were taken off guard and puzzled. If the primary source of the cancer could be found, they would know better how to treat it with chemo in order to give Mom more time.

We wanted time. She wanted time. Mom told us she was not afraid to die, but knowing that she would miss watching her daughters' lives unfold, miss seeing her grandchildren grow up, and miss sharing life with her husband brought deep sorrow. In expressing her sorrow out loud to us, Mom prepared us to hear the truth. The truth was what she explained to me the day the doctors confirmed that there would be no cure. She knew her diagnosis meant death.

I remember diagnosis day well. I drove straight to Mom and Dad's house after work, which had already become the routine. Mom and Dad occasionally said to me, "You don't have to come over every day." They expressed that I should continue living the events of my life. But everything else in my life was on hold. My mother was ill. I wanted every second. I was begging life to stop and stand still for a moment so that I could catch my breath.

Every day brought eight hours of work, and then I went to the house to be with Mom. On that particular day, Mom sat on the couch waiting for me. She had been to her oncologist that afternoon to review the results of the tests and be told what medicine could do or, more importantly, not do for her. Mom knew her daughters inside and out. She knew that I would want every solitary scientific detail before I would begin to officially absorb the reality. I needed Mom's nursing technical version of the information rather than Dad's non-medical terminology.

Mom also knew that I had really already made up my mind. The logical daughter with medical sense, I analyzed upon being told that every lobe of my mother's liver was affected with cancer cells meant a bleak prognosis. I still wanted the science. She knew that. Patiently, she repeated back to me every number, scale, percentage, result, and word the doctor had spoken. She sat on the couch. I sat in the arm chair across from her. I subconsciously chose that seat. Maybe if I created distance between myself and my mother's illness, somehow it would just go away. The nightmare would stop. By the time she neared the end of the explanation my eyes were welled with tears. I was trying hard to keep that flood of sadness from my eyes. She had finished, but left out my one burning question.

"How much time with treatment?" I asked.

"A year, maybe a year and a half," she responded.

I could no longer contain my tears and they spilled over, but what was I supposed to say? I knew that Mom was not afraid to die, so I asked her, "Are you sad?"

Mom began to cry and articulated the same thoughts to me that she had conveyed to my sisters. She was sad that she would miss so much of our lives. "But then I realize," she continued with courage, "that it is all of you who will be doing the missing, not me."

There was my mother, sad, not for herself, but for her girls, her husband, her sons-in-law, her grandchildren. My mother was taking care of her girls first. She knew that it would be heartbreaking to be the ones left behind. She'd be in Heaven. She'd be fine. But her girls, the daughters left to read the emails, we were why she was sad.

From: Pastor Michael Brandt <pastorbrandt@knowingthesavior.org>
To: Family and Friends in Christ
Subject: Jeannie Update 2/15/05

February 15, 2005,

Dear Family and Friends,

The following is a letter I sent in reply to a greeting from Jeannie's coworkers at the SF Surgical Center. I thought you might appreciate some of the info. Thanks for your prayer support.

Dear Rita,

Thanks for the valentine's greeting to Jeannie. Jeannie misses all of you too. She loves her Sioux Falls Surgical Family! You all have been a wonderful encouragement to us. We are blessed to have you, plus our church family, and added to that, a host of friends, who are faithful to pray. What an honor to come before the God of all creation in the Name of His Son, Jesus Christ, knowing that He hears us and answers in the way that is best (1 John 5:14, 15).

In many ways, yesterday had been a good day. Jeannie had an in-home hair cut by one of the members of Abiding Savior, who just happens to be her stylist. Then Ginny Nelson came and helped me out by covering for lunch while I was at the office. The weather permitted us to take a short, lover's stroll. Most days Jeannie has trouble keeping me in line, today she had problems keeping me in step!

In the midst of these good things, the difficulties come with the constant stomach sensation of fullness and discomfort, constant chin (hotspot on the nuclear med bone scan) and back (most likely liver) pain, and general weakness (probably due to Jeannie's lack of calorie intake). In spite of that, Jeannie has a good attitude and a peaceful spirit. God's grace is sufficient (2

Corinthians 12:9). He does not test us beyond what we are able to endure (1 Corinthians 10:13).

We both have some concerns and fears about the unknowns as the chemotherapy starts today…nausea, weakness, headaches, appetite, Port-A-Cath, sensation of chemo, the attached chemo drip bag (at home), etc. In all these things, it is wonderful to know that the Holy Spirit is our Helper. He is a divine counselor who calms our fears and brings to mind the sure promises of God's Word. As Psalm 46:1 declares, "He is a PRESENT help in every time of trouble."

On Valentine's Day, I thank God for the mate He has given me. More than merely the passion and romance of the moment, we have been blessed to experience the bonding, unconditional love of our Heavenly Father. No matter how the world has sought to undermine the value of marriage, the truth remains, marriage is a marvelous blessing entrusted to us by a loving God. The vows Jeannie and I made to one another before Him and the miracle of our oneness in Christ are priceless. For richer or for poorer, for better or for worse, in sickness and in health, until death us do part…this is love. Her person and her loving ways have been sweeter than I could have ever hoped to have. It is my joy to serve her as her helpmate in Christ. If God would grant a miracle of healing, I would be grateful beyond measure. If not, I still will be grateful beyond measure. God has been good to us. Praise be to His Name.

Thanks again for remembering us before the throne of God.

Held in God's Loving Embrace,
Jeannie and Michael

Chapter Eight: I Love Jeannie Because...

Kayla Brandt

None of us knew how to express our deep affection for Mom on Valentine's Day. Death has a way of causing you to take great care in every word spoken, every action portrayed and every moment spent that it might not be wasted. It's disturbing that it often takes the shaking of our world to help us stop, slow down, and contemplate what's really important to us. To consider the reasons we live. Death brought lucidity to our entire family about the brevity of our time on this earth and setting our hopes on higher things. Mom had taught us long before to say "I love you" often and mean it, and now there was never a conversation where we didn't say those words to each other. Mom's love for us was unconditional. It was a constant. Her love embraced us. We wanted Mom to know how much we loved her this Valentine's Day. But our words were suddenly inadequate. They felt like mere syllables that fell short. We all gave heart-felt valentines, and she humbly accepted our outpouring.

Everyone loved Mom. This truly is not an overstatement. She was easy to love. But it was the valentine that arrived from Mom's coworkers at the surgical center that touched us the deepest. I arrived to the house that evening to find an enormous clear glass bowl reflecting in the sunlight that was dripping in through the living room window. Tied to the bowl was a large bouquet of red and pink heart-shaped helium balloons sparkling and dancing in the air. The bowl was filled to its brim and spilling over with white index cards. I reached my hand in and pulled out the first card. Not knowing what to expect, my heart wrenched with sadness and overflowed with joy all at the same time as I read the words, "I love Jeannie because..." I continued to fish index cards out of the bowl. They were filled with thoughtful statements from Mom's coworkers describing why they loved her. And they did. They had taken the time to sit down and reflect on Mom's love for them. The cards told how she touched them, how her smile brightened them, how she brought joy and laughter, how she helped them along their way, how she encouraged them, how she gave them hope. Card upon card echoed, "I love Jeannie because..." It was beautiful. It left me reading and bawling for several hours, but blessed and proud. Proud to call this Jeannie they all loved so much my mom. Our mom, this Jeannie, she was love.

From: Pastor Michael Brandt <pastorbrandt@knowingthesavior.org>
To: Family and Friends in Christ
Subject: Jeannie Update 2/16/05

February 16, 2005,

Dear Family and Friends in Jesus,

God answered another prayer, but not quite like we had hoped. Jeannie has been having a difficult time after the chemo — headache, nausea, and vomiting have been her companions.

Yesterday's treatment was long, but it went well. We arrived at 9 am and left the infusion center at 3:45 pm. Hey, they gave free coffee. I would have stayed even longer. At the surgical center, they give you coffee and fresh bakery goods. I stay there till they're gone. Sadly, due to some selfish cutbacks, the donut count is a little sparse now and then. Or could it be, that the staff (especially the PACU nurses) visits that room too often? Remember, you do not need to take bakery goods in order to find the patient's family.

The second opinion pathology reports from Mayo verified what Dr. Tolentino and the pathologists at Avera had determined. It remains a squamous cell carcinoma without a known primary origin. Jeannie will be having chemo every two weeks (her blood levels will be the determining factor). The third week she will have off. If Jeannie can endure the cycle, then after the second cycle a repeat of the CAT scan will be done. That is scheduled for March 28th the day after Easter. Provided there is a good result (retarding the cancer's growth), we will continue the chemo treatment.

What do we say about these things? When Jeannie was throwing up and I was trying to console her, I said, "God has seen fit to answer our prayer in a way we didn't exactly want." She gave an affirming nod. Then I added, "Well, at least He gives us grace to endure." Hearing my own words, I said, "At least? Why His grace is more than we deserve and it is all that we need." Jeannie, pale as a ghost, quickly agreed. Both of us are understanding better what it means when Paul was told by Christ, "My grace is sufficient for you, for power is perfected in weakness. Most gladly, therefore, I will rather boast about my weaknesses, that the power of Christ may dwell in me." (2 Corinthians 12:9)

God is good. His grace is sufficient. His will is always best. His presence is in us! His glory is our desire.

Thank you for standing with us in prayer. We do not know what tomorrow may bring, but we know God is already in our tomorrow.

At Peace in His Presence,
Jeannie and Michael

P.S. My daughter Erika pointed out that I wrote chin, instead of shin, in my last e-mail. The 'hotspot' is not in her chin, but her shin. I guess all that money for a college education finally paid out! I am also happy to report that an 'old dog' (me) can learn new tricks. I can now distinguish between the beeping of the washing machine and the dryer. By the way, whose idea was it to put the laundry room in the basement? Someone out there could make a 'mint' , if you would just invent a designer couch/washer/dryer combo for the living room.

Chapter Nine: Mom's Sick...

Kayla Brandt

C hemo and radiation began and the floodgates opened. Mom was sick. Chemo made her sicker. We longed to take her place. We wanted to somehow remove her burden, pain, and suffering. We were desperate. Distressed. We knew that only Jesus could do it. It was a hard lesson. She had selflessly put us first our whole lives. She had forever been keenly aware of our needs and desires, and she fulfilled them. We wanted to give back to her all that she had bestowed upon us. Without warning, we were walking into the role of caregivers. But we didn't just walk, we ran to it. Our mother deserved the best. This new role was our desire. And though we were well aware that we were ill-equipped to fill the role, we embraced it. But it was hard. If only we could sacrifice ourselves and take her place.

From: Pastor Michael Brandt <pastorbrandt@knowingthesavior.org>
To: Family and Friends in Christ
Subject: Jeannie Update 2/19/05
February 19, 2005,

Dear Family and Friends,

Psalm 27:5, "For in the day of trouble He will conceal me in His tabernacle; in the secret place of His tent He will hide me; He will lift me up on a rock."

Jeannie and I treasure these wonderful gems of truth. We are sure you do too. No doubt, we have trouble — big time. But we have a big God, bigger than all our troubles. He is covering us, concealing us in the midst of the storm. In His tabernacle, in His secret place, He is hiding Jeannie in His grace. It's not an easy place, but it is a safe place. Notice in the verse above, He doesn't keep us from trouble, but He does conceal us in the midst of it. That was good enough for Joseph in Pharaoh's prison, Daniel in the lion's den, Jesus in the Garden of Gethsemane, and Paul in jail; and it is good enough for Jeannie and me. I hope you would say the same. There is nothing that compares to the secret place of God.

Jeannie has had a tough time of it since receiving the chemo. Nothing wants to stay down, including the meds to stop the nausea. Early this morning (3:30 am) she said, I need to be rehydrated. When the cancer institute opened, in we went. It was a good thing. After the hydration, which was coupled with another anti-nausea med, Dr. Tolentino allowed me to take her back home, as long as I would promise to bring her in again on Saturday and Sunday for more of the same. I said, "You're the doctor." He wears a nametag that says so. He is also concerned about the increase in her headaches, so a MRI is scheduled for Monday. She will also have another x-ray of her left shin. It is more painful by the day. Maybe it will require radiation. The tests will tell.

Just a little sidelight. Many of you know my mother. She is very direct. She uses both a wheelchair and a cane—at the same time. She can really poke that cane around. If you don't believe me, ask my black and blue dad. Due to Jeannie's shin, I bought her a stylin' cane. Today when I was wheeling Jeannie from our car to the doctor's office, as we approached the elevator, Jeannie said, "Let me do a 'Lorraine'." She proceeded to whip out her new cane and punch the elevator button. It scared me. I don't want to be married to my mother!

Thank you for your faithful concern. God is truly keeping us in His care. Have no doubts, when we are down, we will let you know, so you can pray more specifically. Sometimes it happens quickly. One moment a heaviness sets in, but like an updraft of wind, the Spirit of God lifts us up. It is amazing. It is all due to His amazing loving kindness, mercy, and grace. Keep praying - for us and for others. We are doing the same.

Hiding In His Secret Place and Standing on the Rock, JESUS! (By the way, if you haven't surrendered to Jesus, there is room in His secret place for you.)

Jeannie and Michael

P.S. Another first - I blow dried Jeannie's hair today. How can those beauticians live with themselves, when they charge those outrageous prices? It took me about two shakes of a tornado. Now, I'm not saying I did as good a job as they would do, but with today's 'look', who would know. Anyway, Jeannie looks good even with 'bed hair'!

Chapter Ten: Ministering to the Minister...

Kayla Brandt

Alisha bore the brunt of the burden. Her schedule was quickly rearranged, allowing her to quit her in-home job as a medical transcriptionist in order to free up her days to take care of Mom. This arrangement allowed Dad a few hours every day to maintain his role as shepherd of the church. Many were hurting, and Mom again put others first by seeing the importance of Dad continuing to serve his parish.

Dad was a minister to so many. He was the shepherd of God's flock at Abiding Savior. But his wife was hurting. His daughters were hurting. He was hurting. But how could he stop to nurse his wounds? Dad knew that there was an entire congregation hurting and needing comfort, as well. God granted Dad the grace throughout Mom's entire illness to preach pure and effective messages to his congregation. He continued to minister to the church even as its members attempted to minister to him. Dad displayed complete strength, the kind that only God can give, throughout the entire trial

At the beginning, caregiving meant taking Mom to doctor appointments, chemo and radiation treatments, and sitting with her while she rested. They were days of precious alone time with Mom. But the tranquil waters quickly vanished as the rushing side effects of chemo began to roll in.

---- ✉ ----

From: Pastor Michael Brandt <pastorbrandt@knowingthesavior.org>
To: Family and Friends in Christ
Subject: Jeannie Update 2/23/05
February 23, 2005,

Dear Family and Friends,

As most of you have heard, Jeannie's first chemo was a little difficult. However, God is faithful and He provides sufficient grace for each step of the way. Some of those steps were mighty quick, as Jeannie headed to the bathroom. It's miserable to go through, many of you have suffered through these same trials and worse. In the midst of it all, Jeannie is grateful that you have been remembering her in prayer and says, "Thank you." Please don't forget, prayer does not simply enable us to do great work for God, PRAYER IS THE GREAT WORK!

Due to the chemo's aftermath, we had to forgo the family photo session which had been scheduled for Friday am. Ben and Ona had come down from Grand Forks, ND for the planned family photo. This was the first we had seen them, since Jeannie was diagnosed with cancer. Like Ona said, "Seeing mom so ill, moved the 'bad dream' into the realm of reality." It also confirmed the fact, that Jesus enables us to meet every reality in His strength.

Yesterday (Tuesday, February 22nd), Jeannie had her second round of chemo. The MRI of Jeannie's head, the shin x-ray, and blood tests taken on Monday had all been read by Dr. Tolentino. He prescribed a different chemo recipe (less apt to cause nausea) and also scheduled hydration coupled with an anti-nausea med for the remaining days of this week and three days next week. Hopefully, this will help lessen the negative effects of the chemo.

Dr. T said the MRI revealed there was 'nothing' in Jeannie's head! Now from a cancer point of view that was good news, but what does it say about her IQ? In fact, what does it say about the quality of education received at St. Olaf College, where Jeannie graduated summa cum laude with a degree in nursing! Furthermore, what does it say about Sioux Falls Surgical Center's standard for hiring nurses (I've heard Jeannie was one of the 'brighter' ones)? If you can attain a 4 point grade average at St. Olaf without anything in your head, then my 2.8 grade average from the Univ. of MN must put me in the genius range, because my academic advisor told me my head was full of rocks. Go Gophers!

The x-ray of her left shin did reveal an active cancerous growth. It has eaten into the bone and runs the risk of causing further damage (possible brake to the tibia), if not treated with radiation. Dr. T referred us to Dr. Griffen in the oncology radiation wing of the Avera Cancer Institute. After reading the x-rays and examining Jeannie, he prescribed radiation treatments that will last for approximately ten days. Those treatments will begin today. Because the hydration and the radiation are given in the same building, Jeannie's appointments will be scheduled one after the other.

"How are you doing?" This is a question we are often asked. It reveals a genuine concern and we appreciate being asked. By the grace of God, He is holding on to us. The other day, someone told me to 'hang in there'. I knew what they meant, but in all truth I can't. No one can. Left to handle these trials on our own, the strongest of us would finally reach the breaking point. But God can and does hold those who call upon Him in the Name of His one and only Son, Jesus. Isn't that great news?! How are Jeannie and I doing? Well, we're in His grip ... at peace, sometimes nervous, mostly able to sleep, joyful (even when shedding tears) ... BUT ALWAYS IN HIS GRIP!

Did you know that He has never dropped anything? In John 10:27,28 Jesus says, "My sheep hear My voice, and I know them, and they follow me; and I give eternal life to them, and they shall never perish; and no one shall snatch them out of My hand." Years ago Jeannie and I heard Jesus calling us to come to Him. By His grace, we did and we have followed Him. We are confident that He is holding us. I hope you've asked Him to take hold of your life. Like Jeannie and me, you need Him, for you too were born a sinner and have sinned. Don't wait until something disastrous happens, surrender your life to Him now. You'll never regret doing so, for His nail pierced hand is gentle with forgiveness and strong enough to hold you forever.

In His Grip,
Jeannie and Michael

P.S. I have had it rough in those waiting rooms. Receptionists control the remote controls for the TVs. It is inhuman to make anyone watch Ophra!

Chapter Eleven: Calming the Storm...

Kayla Brandt

Once Mom began chemotherapy, our lives spiraled out of control in a hurry. The vomiting was intense and explosive. Headaches were constant. Mom couldn't eat. She couldn't drink. She couldn't sleep. Every slight smell made her nauseated. She was weak and in pain on a consistent basis. She was deteriorating. Chemo was supposed to be making her better, slowing down the growth of the cancer. All we could see was our mother becoming more sick and more miserable.

Usually alone, Alisha bore the burden of watching her mother suffer day in and day out. Often when Mom was throwing up Alisha would leave the bathroom for just a moment in fear that she would throw up, too. She'd rush down to the kitchen sink to wet a washcloth with cool water to place on Mom's head and neck. Standing there at the kitchen sink, Alisha cried where Mom couldn't see her. Hurriedly, she'd brush the tears away, take a deep breath, and race back up to the bathroom to try to carry Mom through each treacherous episode. Alisha bathed Mom, blow dried her hair, brushed her teeth, sat with her, and prepared meals and shakes that she had to beg Mom to swallow.

Alisha was a consistent presence. Her structured common sense allowed her to organize and handle the daily details of Mom's schedule and care. She calmed the storm. Some of these days were filled with talking and laughter, recalling memories, and expressing dreams and hopes. Other days the plight was too difficult and Mom and Alisha would just sit together in pensive silence. Alisha possessed the ability to see and anticipate Mom's next need, which brought peace and security to Mom.

From: Pastor Michael Brandt <pastorbrandt@knowingthesavior.org>
To: Family and Friends in Christ
Subject: Jeannie Update 2/24/05

February 24, 2005

Dear Family and Friends,

Last night Jeannie and I rejoiced in Psalm 30. Take time to read it. We have enjoyed praying the Psalms back to God ... "In the midst of our days, we extol you our God and our Healer. We thank and praise Your name forever. Yes, Your anger is for a moment, but Your favor is for a lifetime. Weeping may last for the night, but joy comes in the morning. O Lord, by Thy favor Thou hast enabled us to stand. We will declare your faithfulness. O Lord our God, we will give thanks to Thee forever. In Jesus Name, Amen."

Just a quick report and request for prayer, plus a comment. Jeannie rejoices that the nausea, from yesterday's chemo treatment, has been less than last week's aftermath. She and I thank you for praying. We are also happy to report that the first radiation treatment went well. Would you pray for her appetite to return? Her energy is gone. She's being hydrated, but she needs to take in some calories. I've tried to set a good example (note my calorie intake), but so far she has not had any desire to eat and nothing I suggest sounds good. Pray that she will be able to just do it. Once again, we ask you to expand your prayer covering to others who are also battling serious health concerns.

Now, for what it is worth. My daughter Erika drew my attention to two mistakes she found in my last update. First, she indicated that I spelled 'brake', when it should have been break. "Big deal," I said. Secondly, she said, "It is Oprah, not Ophra." My response was, "Erika, didn't you read that I only received a 2.8 grade point average from Gofigure U in Minnesota... and not only that, I wrote that update at 11 pm. I was exhausted... and besides, you have a degree in education from Northwestern College with summa cum laude honors...and you were a teacher." And she said, "Dad, I taught first grade!" A guy just can't win in this house of women. As soon as this is sent, she'll find some 'heir'. I'm sure of it!

Proud to be Fools for Christ,
Jeannie and Michael

Chapter Twelve: He Knows the Way I Take...

Kayla Brandt

Through the hardships, Mom never complained. Rather, she was busy thinking of everyone else. Mom, together with Alisha's help, set herself to the tasks of preparation. She had birthday cards bought for months in advance that needed to be written on. Father's Day cards that had been purchased and tucked away needed to be pulled out now. There were birthday and wedding presents to plan. Mom even unveiled a secret hiding place where a delicate stuffed lamb lay to be given upon birth to the new grandbaby Erika was carrying. Alisha was shocked. She had known for years that Mom was organized, but Mom's determined preparation washed wonder over Alisha.

"What an extraordinary mother we are about to lose," Alisha thought.

During the hours Mom was tucked away in bed for naps, Alisha's tears were released. The hard crying was saved for the haven of the car. Most of the drives home every day involved a phone call to either me or Erika to give an update on Mom's condition and the events of the day. Vocalizing what she had watched Mom endure brought out sympathetic sorrow within Alisha. She wept and begged God to ease Mom's pain. Her fears poured out in sobs to her sisters along with doubts of her ability to continue on.

"I can't do this," Alisha told us. "I can't go back and watch her suffer. Why is this happening? I can't do this…" her voice trailed off.

Alisha watched Mom suffer. Over and over and over again. It was torture – like some strange punishment God was giving us. God used Job 23:10 to soften our hurt, "But He knows the way I take; when He has tried me, I shall come forth as gold." Despite the hardships, God granted Alisha the next measure of strength to press on as she tenderly mothered her own mom. There was no one better to do it. Alisha's steady and unwavering hand in Mom's care spoke volumes of the daily strength God gives us when we face heartache.

He knows the way we take.

And He makes us come forth like gold.

From: Pastor Michael Brandt <pastorbrandt@knowingthesavior.org>
To: Family and Friends in Christ
Subject: Jeannie Update 3/6/05

March 6, 2005

Dear Family and Friends in Jesus,

Jeannie and I thank you for your faithfulness to pray for us. The fellowship of believers in Christ is just that, fellows-in-the-same-ship of faith. Whether the sea of life is calm or stormy, the joy of having shipmates who pull together is wonderful.

Jeannie has been receiving radiation on her leg and hydration this week. For the most part, the week has gone better. However, as you can imagine, the number of narcotics and other meds Jeannie is taking have their own unique side effects and complications. You can't live without them, and living with them is sometimes a challenge. Under their influence, a dizzy blonde can even get a little dizzier. We've had a couple of falls, but no injuries. That is why your praying for Jeannie is such a blessing. God is good and His grace is sufficient.

Next week Jeannie begins another round of chemo. We meet with a new oncologist, Dr. Sanjeevi. He is filling in for Dr. Tolentino. Please pray that we might be a good witness to him. Jeannie and I know that God wants us to always reflect Christ to those we encounter on this journey.

Most of you know that chemo seeks to kill bad cells. In the process there is the odor of death. Jeannie and I desire to be the fragrance of life in the midst of this trial. The Holy Spirit states it so well through the words of the Apostle Paul, "For we are a fragrance of Christ to God among those who are being saved and among those who are perishing." (2 Corinthians 2:15) If the stench of death is choking you, simply do two things. First, exhale sin's deadly effects by admitting and confessing your sins to Jesus (simply ask Him to forgive you). Then inhale, ask Jesus to come into your heart with His life giving presence. When you breath deeply of Jesus, not even cancer's deadly effects can steal away the joy of your eternal life in Christ.

Now on the lighter side... In these last weeks, Jeannie has discovered that over the years, I've held out on her concerning my abilities in the domestic department. She has now discovered I can do the bedding on three beds, wash an additional four loads of clothes (even with proper separating of colors and fold the same), cook three meals (okay, re-heat three meals), write thank you notes, and still have plenty of time to watch the outdoor channel. But wait a second, I too have learned something. Anyone can wash all the windows of our home, inside and out, in an hour and a half. How is that possible? Just call Shawn at ACE Window Cleaning! And to think, all these years, Jeannie made me feel her washing windows was a BIG deal.

Breathing Deeply In Jesus,
Jeannie and Michael

Chapter Thirteen: Anticipation...

Kayla Brandt

Then there was Erika.

Her quandary was deep. The weeks of Mom's illness became a burden she was forced to silently bear most days all by herself. Shortly after Mom was diagnosed, there was more news to tell. It was wonderful news in the midst of our family's sorrow, but a source of grief as well. Erika was three months pregnant, bearing her third child. We were overjoyed at the expectation of new life, but for Mom, the knowledge that she would probably never hold this child in her arms caused a mixture of joy and sadness. Erika's past two pregnancies had been fraught with multiple complications, and this one was no different. By March, Erika's doctor ordered her to total bed rest. It was a difficult order and one that she did not want to follow. She had two energetic toddlers to care for, the responsibilities of a wife, and her mother was dying of cancer. Erika perhaps had the most time to contemplate what was to come. She was the one left to think and ponder. Family members, friends, and people in the church stepped in to help her care for her two children and her household. Meals, laundry, cleaning, babysitting were just a few of the services offered. It was necessary assistance for Erika to receive, but it left her very lonely.

From: Pastor Michael Brandt <pastorbrandt@knowingthesavior.org>
To: Family and Friends in Christ
Subject: Jeannie Update 3/18/05

March 18, 2005,

Dear Family and Friends in Christ,

Psalm 27:13-14, "I would have despaired unless I had believed that I would see the goodness of the Lord in the land of the living. Wait for the Lord; be strong, and let your heart take courage; yes, wait for the Lord."

The last couple of weeks have been a challenge. As I mentioned in the last update, Jeannie received chemo, hydration, and a blood transfusion on March 8th. Even though the chemo wasn't as harsh, she kept getting weaker — no appetite and difficulties keeping food down. Last Monday, March 14th, after her 14th and final radiation treatment, Jeannie had a blood draw to determine if she could have chemo the next day.

Her levels were lower than before, so they gave her another unit of blood. A two–hour transfusion turned in to a 6.5 hour ordeal. In spite of the frustrations, Jeannie maintained a sweet, understanding spirit. That was a great witness to me. I shut my mouth and wrote 45 thank you notes, while we waited! The following day (March 15th), the Dr. felt she was too weak to have another treatment. They gave her hydration and sent us home. He scheduled Jeannie to come in on March 22nd for another evaluation. At that time, he will determine if she can continue.

Since Tuesday, things have continued about the same. Her leg (shin) pain is about a level 2. Praise God, we believe the radiation has helped. Her pain in the area of her liver has remained at a level 2 to 5. Now she is having increased pain in her abdomen (level 4 to 5). She continues using the pain patch and has increased her oxycodone. Irregularity is another problem. She does not complain, but has said she hopes this will not continue too long. Yet, the goodness of God enables her to endure and even overcome the setbacks.

In the midst of it all, Jeannie and I are experiencing many blessings. Closeness to one another, closeness with you, our family and friends, and most of all a greater closeness to Jesus. His nearness keeps us from despair. Strange as it may seem to those who have not surrendered to Christ, trials draw a child of God deeper into His eternal, loving embrace. As the hymn writer declared, "Every day with Jesus is sweeter than the day before!"

Everything in life has a deeper meaning to you. For example, last Wednesday, March 16th, Erika and Kayla helped Jeannie's weakened body into the car. They drove her to church, where the bell choir, Jeannie had organized and directed, was set to play for the Lenten Service. I met them at the door with a wheelchair. We kept well-wishers at arm's length. The bell choir played, the congregation sang, Jeannie joyfully wept. Then the girls whisked her away, back to our home. She was exhausted, but refreshed in spirit. She said, "That was the best bell number ever!" It was. Not because they played it flawlessly, but because trials cause you to appreciate such blessings all the more. You no longer take them for granted. You no longer pick them apart. You simply receive them from God and praise His Name, thanking Him for those who have served Him and you. Could it be that more trials are needed to draw us nearer to Him? Moms and dads need to teach their children such truths. If you don't, Satan will use the same trials to make you bitter rather than better.

Now, I do have a bone to pick with Jeannie. Why didn't she stay for my message? She would have been able to say, "That was the best message I've ever heard!" On second thought, it may take more trials than anyone could ever endure for that to be said. I can hear all of you, especially Jeannie's PACU buddies at the Surgical Center, saying, "Amen, Brother."

I want to leave you with one closing thought from the writings of C.S. Lewis, "We are not necessarily doubting that God will do the best for us; we are only wondering how painful the best will turn out to be." Jeannie and I know it will not be more painful than His grace can handle.

Drawing Closer and Closer to Jesus,
Jeannie and Michael Brandt

Chapter Fourteen: Filling the Gap...

Kayla Brandt

One can only sit and think in silence for so long about what is to come before the weight of it becomes distressing. Without the distractions of work, Erika's mind wandered often to the dreaded anticipation of losing her mom. It gave her almost too much time to prepare. Added to this weight was the guilt of physically not being able to care for her mother. Stress hovered over Erika like a dark cloud. The glaring realities were blinding and angered her. How much bigger was this trial going to get? How much more did God think she could handle? Erika cried out and pleaded along with the prophet Isaiah, "It is enough, God. It is enough." Yet, Erika trusted her Savior's sovereign control. She prayed for and waited upon His measure of mercy and grace, and it was delivered.

Erika is a story teller. She speaks with animation. We have often joked that Erika telling the story takes longer than the events actually took to occur; but how delightful it is to listen to her. Erika's unique way with speech was one of the greatest cares delivered to Mom. She came over to the house to sit and visit with Mom every chance she had. Those story-filled hours brought essential breaks in Mom's monotonous and agonizing days. Erika would have traded her bed-ridden situation in a heartbeat to have the opportunity to provide hands-on caregiving to Mom, but this was not God's plan. Instead, Erika conveyed the trivial day-to-day humors and events with a plethora of detail. Her stories kept Mom from feeling distant and withdrawn from this life. Mom wasn't waiting to die, she was living. But when you're as sick as Mom was, you are stripped of your capacity to be an active participant in the routines of life. We take it for granted. Erika gave Mom the immense pleasure of staying in the moments. She filled the gap. She kept things normal, and that was good.

From: Pastor Michael Brandt <pastorbrandt@knowingthesavior.org>
To: Family and Friends in Christ
Subject: Jeannie Update 3/23/05

March 23, 2005,

Dear Family and Friends in Christ,

John 11:3, "The sisters (Mary and Martha) therefore sent to Jesus, saying, 'Lord, behold, the one, whom You love, is sick.'" Even though this was said about Lazarus, I believe Jeannie, and each one who trusts in Jesus, can take these words to heart. Could a better word be said about you than, "the one, whom Jesus loves ..."? Think about it. Jesus loved Lazarus, yet He permitted him to not only be ill, but to die. Then, Jesus came and raised him up from the dead as verse 4 states, "for the glory of God, that the Son may be glorified by it." Lazarus was raised up from the dead. His life became a testimony to the Divinity of Jesus. Afterwards, Lazarus had to endure great criticism, even threats of death, from those who hated Jesus. Finally, he passed away again. Difficult to understand? Maybe to some, but to me it is enough that it was said of Lazarus, "the one, whom Jesus loved, ...". In fact, Jeannie and I love Him because He first loved us. We hope you have come to love Him too. Take a moment to read 1 John 4:7-21.

Jesus loves Jeannie. He knows she is sick. He has a plan. We pray for healing. Without a doubt, we know He can heal her. We are equally confident, that His will is best, best for His glory and best for Jeannie's good. It is more than comforting to know and to say, "the one (Jeannie), whom You love, is sick." It is enough to know He loves her, He loves me, He loves our children and grandchildren. What could be more assuring? It drives the doubts away.

Today, Dr. Tolentino saw Jeannie and reviewed her progress. After sharing his thoughts and observations with us, it was decided to discontinue further chemo treatments. The evidence does not indicate any significant good is being accomplished. At the same time, there is evidence that each treatment is making Jeannie's overall condition worse by both weakening her and, at the same time, causing her great discomfort. Jeannie agreed with Dr. Tolentino's assessment. He also suggested we, under his supervision, begin the process of contacting hospice care. Jeannie and I concurred with him. We notified our children and, as a family, plan to meet with inhome hospice care this Friday. We know God will give us His clear leading on the way hospice can best serve Jeannie's ongoing needs. Please continue to pray for us. We want to be a witness to each of those associated with hospice care.

Hard news? Yes, indeed. Many tears have been shed. Even Dr. Tolentino wept with us. We love him. Then, he humbly prayed for God's miraculous intervention. Through it all, Jeannie and I have sensed God's presence and His peace. Our girls have also revealed the remarkable strength God provides. In the midst of their frustration and extreme sadness, they have openly shared their confidence in God's higher ways.

Thank you for your continuing encouragement. You have been a fulfillment of Galatians 6:2, "Share each others troubles and problems and thus fulfill the love of Christ."

May Easter's resurrection victory encourage all of us. Because He lives, we can face tomorrow!

Jeannie didn't waste a moment in making the most of this new situation. While sitting down stairs this evening, I mentioned something I wanted to do. She quickly over-ruled my suggesting by simply saying, "You will have plenty of time to do it your way after I'm gone." End of discussion. I started to protest that tactic and she gave me her 'look'. And to think, some of you have felt sorry for her all these years. Why, she has always held the 'trump card'. You know what? I wouldn't have had it any other way, not before and not now!!

It is getting late. I'm not going to proof read this update. If you find some mistakes in spelling or grammar, give yourself a pat on the back! You deserve it.

From Two, Who Know Jesus Loves Us, Jeannie and Michael

Till death do us part, April 5, 1969

Jeannie, one month before diagnosis, December 2004

Even a picnic needs
to be pretty! Jeannie
and her girls. 1986

Michael & Jeannie,
Niagara Falls, 2002

We love our Mom & Gramma! (back: Darryl, Alisha, Kayla, Erika, Sherwin; front: Mom on couch, Isabelle, Emma Wesley, Isaac)

Jeannie Brandt,
one month before
diagnosis

**Kayla, third daughter
and co-author**

**Jeannie and her girls, Easter 2005
(back: Ona, Erika, Alisha; front: Mom and Kayla)**

Papa Mike and
grandkids, June 2005

Chapter Fifteen: A Well-Tuned Ear...

Kayla Brandt

A s much as Erika talks, she is also a born listener. Her ears are well-tuned to another's hardship. She became a buffer for the rest of us girls. There were daily conversations on the phone, some into the wee hours of the night. Erika listened intently to Alisha and I cry about the tragic setbacks we witnessed as Mom's health steadily declined. She encouraged us to continue on no matter how hard it was to watch our mother suffer. She eased our natural feelings of guilt when we thought we couldn't handle anymore. What felt like weakness to us wasn't really, it was just plain real and hard. Erika understood it was strenuous to be the caregivers and that we felt inadequate when we wanted just a short break. How could we? How could we want to get away from it? But Erika intelligently explained it wasn't that we wanted to get away, but rather, we wanted Mom's suffering to go away. And Erika listened to Ona. Being miles away, Ona felt the similar agony of Erika. They couldn't help. The cross they bore was the distance between what was tangible and intangible. But we were family – we stopped and helped each other walk along the road.

From: Pastor Michael Brandt <pastorbrandt@knowingthesavior.org>
To: Family and Friends in Christ
Subject: Jeannie Update 3/28/05

Michael Brandt

March 28, 2005,

Dear Family and Friends in Christ,

"But now Christ has been raised from the dead, the first fruits of those who are asleep," 1 Corinthians 15:20.

Praise God for the Resurrection! The greatest Hope known to those who believe in Jesus. Every issue in life, from the believer's salvation to his suffering, finds its resolution in the Resurrection.

Jesus is alive. He is alive in Jeannie and me. Many years ago, we heard Him knocking on our heart's door (Revelation 3:20). We asked Him to come in as our Savior and Lord. Because He lives, we can face tomorrow. Because He lives in us, our tomorrows extend into an everlasting eternity with Him in Heaven. Sin's power is broken. Sickness does not have the final say. The devil can't scare us or claim us. Death and the grave cannot hold us. We have the Resurrection, Jesus Christ, living in us! Does He live in you? He is waiting for you to ask Him.

Now you know why Jeannie and I are full of Hope, a sure and living Hope, the Hope of the ages. A Hope that keeps us praying for a temporary miracle, Jeannie's healing. A Hope that has already provided the greatest miracle, our salvation unto life everlasting. We are in a win, win situation. Two hopeless losers, that were made winners by the grace and mercy of Christ. The victory of His empty cross and His empty tomb have provided us with the fullness of Hope. A Hope we long to fully realize at His appearing! Do you have this Hope? He is yours for the asking.

As I mentioned in the last update, Jeannie is now in-home hospice care. On Good Friday, we met both our primary hospice nurse, Michelle, and our social worker, Candice. They were so kind and gracious as they explained hospice care. Michelle shared her faith in Christ with us. As time goes on, we will be using their services more and more. Jeannie and I would like Jeannie to stay at home until Jesus heals her or takes her to Glory. All four of our daughters were able to be included in that meeting. It helps when all of us are hearing and understanding the same information. Our girls have been so good to us. But then, they had a great teacher and example in their mother.

Jeannie continues to weaken. Lately, her pain and discomfort levels have been intense. Restless nights and uncomfortable days have taken their toll. Her care is one of balancing many issues: pain, medicines and their side effects, appetite, energy, sleep, etc. I'm learning a great deal about each one of them. However, when I get a little too bossy, Jeannie reminds me that I do not have a license to practice medicine. She may be weaker physically, but her spunk has not diminished one bit. In fact, the other day I was making her walk around the house, with my help of course. We were having some trouble negotiating the steps. She was tipping, bumping into me. So I said, "You seem a little more unsteady today." Without a moments hesitation she snapped, "You seem a little wider!" O well, I just reminded her that I'm the one who dispenses the meds and I won't be LAX about it, if you know what I mean.

Thank you for being so faithful to remember us in prayer and with acts of kindness. Jeannie's workplace, the Sioux Falls Surgical Center, has done more that anyone would ever imagine. One of the nurses made a quilt for Jeannie. The quilt was made available for a matching gift raffle with Thrivent Financial. Today a check and the quilt were given to Jeannie. Thanks to their generosity, many of our out of pocket expenses will be covered. The guilt and the thoughtfulness of fellow workers have wrapped Jeannie up in love. Those who encourage others are part of the silver lining in back of life's blackest storm clouds.

Eternally Alive in Christ Jesus,
Jeannie and Michael

Chapter Sixteen: Important Moments...

Kayla Brandt

Little Ona. The baby. That's how we always thought of our fourth-born sister. Ona had never done anything to earn the reputation of being the baby, but we all treated her as one. She was the youngest. We affectionately called her Lil' O and Ona Bologna. She was grown, mature, married, self-sufficient, smart, and independent, but she had always been the baby and will forever remain that way in our eyes. We have an instinct to protect her. So did our mother. We all babied the baby.

When Mom became ill, Ona had a tough time of it. The distance between Sioux Falls and Grand Forks turned from a short four and one-half hour drive into a massive abyss. A canyon. It seemed like an insurmountable divide. But God provided again. He permitted Ona and Benjy to travel to Sioux Falls with precision explainable only by the hand of God. They experienced Mom on good days and bad. God in His grace allowed them to be present for the most critical and crucial moments.

One of those important moments, though it may seem silly to most, was being here for the annual Easter egg hunt. Every year, Mom and Dad went through painstaking efforts and late night hours to plan our Easter egg hunt. We girls looked forward to the hunt with gleeful and giddy anticipation. Pathetically, we did not grow out of it and requested Easter egg hunts even as grown teenagers in high school. Hey, it was no ordinary event. Each hunt was a progressive series of rhyming clues leading you to the next clue and the next, ending with your colorful basket filled with treats and treasures. We adult children had finally forfeited our pleasure, but Mom carried the tradition on to her grandchildren.

This year, with Mom being sick, Ona, Benjy, and I grouped together to accomplish the task. The three of us journeyed to Wal-Mart to collect the goodies and came home with a colorful display of eggs, treats, and toys. Mom helped us stuff eggs and prepare the baskets and then gave us helpful hints on how to write clues. She was too weak and medicated to write the clues herself, but she watched on with guidance and a bright smile.

"Pick the place you are going to hide the clue first, and then write the rhyme around it," she wisely advised.

We struggled. We found out we were not poets. Mom ventured to bed but the three of us continued on late into the night as Mom and Dad had often done for us girls. I am quite sure that we had never laughed as hard as we did that night. Benjy's rhymes were the worst, and I don't mind saying so. Ona and Benjy's distance from the rest of us was again a reminder about time. We did not waste it, did not take it for granted. We relished in every moment spent together with our mom.

From: Pastor Michael Brandt <pastorbrandt@knowingthesavior.org>
To: Family and Friends in Christ
Subject: Jeannie Update 4/5/05

April 5, 2005,

Dear Family and Friends in Christ,

"When I remember Thee on my bed, I meditate on Thee in the night watches, For Thou hast been my help, and in the shadow of Thy wings I sing for joy. My soul clings to Thee; Thy right hand upholds me," Psalm 63:6-8.

When you are going through a trial, especially illness, days and nights blend together. Though you are tired and seemingly rest much of the time, sleep is hard to come by. It's hard to know if it is day or night, let alone what day of the week it is. Sometimes you'd rather it was night, at least then the frustration of feeling useless isn't so pronounced. A day usually starts with needing help to get up, looking for someone or something to steady your walk, trying to eat a little something, attempting to keep some pills down, hoping the digestive track kicks into gear or slows down (whatever the dilemma), seeking a somewhat comfortable position, accepting changing body temps (cold one minute, hot the next), coming to grips with the effects the drugs have on your eyes (dim is best) and ears (a hollow ring), and finally assessing the level of discomfort inorder to keep ahead of the curve when it comes to pain. From a caregiver's point of view, I just feel bad that someone I love is going through these unavoidable steps. At the same time, I marvel at Jeannie's uncomplaining attitude and grateful spirit. In fact, in some of the most difficult times, Jeannie has broken forth with praise and adoration for the Lord. Oh, how that has helped me. There is no doubt the Spirit of God is providing grace sufficient for the moment, just like Jesus said He would.

It has now been one week since Jeannie has officially been in in-home hospice care. I am happy to say that the last 3 days have really been good days. Jeannie has been able to eat a little more normally, the digestive track is working much better, the pain levels are under control, Jeannie is able to sleep for longer stretches (me too!), she has been able to focus and read some of your cards, and she's been a little feisty. Why the change? One of our doctors said, it is probably due to the chemo working its way through and out of Jeannie's system. I remain hopeful for a miracle and at the same time continue to face the situation in a realistic manner. God is sovereign and in control. We would not want it to be any other way. We are grateful for better days and a more normal way to spend time with our children, grandchildren, and extended family. Amidst the necessary naps, we try to make use of every available moment.

The caregiving by our daughters, friends, and hospice workers has been exceptional. The kindness shown to us in prayer support, food, cards, e-mails, flowers, and calls has been uplifting. We deeply appreciate your expressions of love and care.

Today is our 36th wedding anniversary. I learned a hard lesson in the card section at Lewis Drug Store last week. They don't make anniversary cards for couples facing a terminal illness. Each of the cards had thankful memories of the wedding day. They all had memories of days since, "We said, I do." The problem came with their next thoughts, thoughts of years to come. At this point, I swallowed hard. Then the thought quickly came, "Michael, don't miss celebrating this anniversary, by looking at days you've never been promised." Therefore, this one will be the best one ever. Why? Because it is one more God has graciously given to us. For better, for worse; for richer, for poorer; in sickness, and in health ... they have all been wonderful. Yes, this one most of all. I praise God for each day He has given us under the banner of His love and grace. Companion, mate, lover, life partner, and dearest friend; all in one person I call Jeannie Marie. Thank you, Jesus!

In church this past Sunday, I said we've been married 37 years. Don't worry, my daughters have already corrected me. Yes, they have also joined many of you in placing a 'GUILT' trip on me for writing guilt, instead of quilt, in my last e-mail. You people are merciless. Don't you have anything better to do? From now on, when you find a word spelled incorrectly, a mistake in grammar, or any other goof, consider it a test. Yes, I am testing you, 'know it all' types. That should take some wind out of your SALES! ... or is it, sails? ... not as easy as you thought, is it?

Two Lovers Still Holding Hands, While in the Palm of God's Hand,
Jeannie and Michael

Chapter Seventeen: Role Reversal...

Kayla Brandt

A nd then there was me.

The third daughter. Care giving took on a very personal meaning to me. You see, a significant bond developed between Mom and me ten years earlier when I required her delicate care. It was a head-on car accident that drove me bruised and battered into Mom's healing arms. The accident left me very broken – physically, emotionally, mentally, and spiritually. Mom saw my need. She prayed for me hard and often. She always prayed for all of her girls, but for me there was a constant prayer that I would come to the cross. I hadn't fully claimed the forgiveness of the cross and she knew this.

Mom recalled without any hesitation the phone call she received the day I should have died. I had just arrived at the emergency room in Willmar, Minnesota, and there was a rush of commotion as doctors and nurses tried to attend to my most life threatening injuries. I was a minor and they needed to at least try to obtain parental permission to treat me. Amazingly, God's grace allowed me to remember and verbalize our home phone number. Mom was home and answered the call. The words she received were blunt, but vague. Her daughter had been in a car accident. Had several broken bones. Was it alright to treat me? And they should come.

Mom had many questions, but the answers were not to come then. As a nurse she knew that if she could hear my voice it would give her insight into the severity of my condition. As a mother she knew that her daughter needed to hear her voice. She asked that the phone be taken to me in the ER. The staff obliged her request and the phone was gingerly placed next to my ear. I could hear her. She brought calm.

What did she hear? She heard gurgled, muffled moans from my voice. She knew upon those sounds that I was critical.

What did I hear? I remember it well and will never forget. "Call out to Jesus, Kayla. I love you and am coming. Call out to Jesus."

She was pleading with me. She knew my need of salvation, and now, faced with the risk that I was about to be taken, she longed for me to have the assurance of a heavenly eternity.

Mom and Dad rushed to the car and traveled through blizzard conditions to get to me. They arrived at the hospital, and from then on Mom never left my side. She was with me literally twenty-four hours a day, seven days a week. She carried me through the intense and unpredictable moments of danger while I was in the intensive care unit, the endless recovery time in the hospital, the multitude of surgeries to repair my broken body, agonizing rehab and therapy sessions, and countless doctor appointments. Mom stood right there next to me through it all.

Now, she was sick and broken. It was my time to give back to her the gentle and tender care she had poured over me. She brought me hope when I was weary and now I desired to do the same for her.

From: Pastor Michael Brandt <pastorbrandt@knowingthesavior.org>
To: Family and Friends in Christ
Subject: Jeannie Update 4/20/05

April 20, 2005

Dear Family and Friends in Christ,

Last night Jeannie and I shared Psalm 84. Verse 11 stood out to us, "For the Lord God is a sun and shield; the Lord gives grace and glory; No good thing does He withhold from those who walk uprightly."

There is no doubt, Jesus is our sun. He lights the way for us. His presence warms our hearts in the cold realities of life. The Son of God is the Light that has come into the world. In fact, by faith Jeannie and I have received Him into our lives. His holiness has driven away the cold, darkness of our sin.

He is also our shield. Ephesians 6:16 speaks of the shield of faith that extinguishes the flaming missiles (attacks) of the evil one. It is true, when you are physically weak, Satan bombards you. He relentlessly fires missiles of fear, doubt, and guilt. But praise God, the shield of childlike faith in Jesus quenches every one of them. Now that is total health coverage, spiritual health included! Why, He even paid the deductible.

Each new day, Christ bestows on us His grace and glory. His grace is new every morning. Leftovers may be good, when it comes to food, but when it comes to God's mercies and lovingkindness, they are always fresh. Great is His faithfulness. This is where His glory is found. If you want to be surrounded by the glory of God, simply rest in the center of His will and grace. Jesus did, even on the Cross of Calvary!

Now comes the crowning promise, NO GOOD THING will He withhold from those who walk uprightly. Jeannie and I are grateful to declare, "This is true." Jesus is the One who has made us upright. We were born downright, dirty sinners. By His shed blood, He has washed us and made us upright, clean believers. Day by day, the Holy Spirit enables us to walk uprightly. He has not withheld any good things from us, not even His healing power. Each day we see His healing hand of mercy. One day we will be made perfectly whole, when we see Him face to face.

This is full recovery! We trust this is your hope too.

I can hear some of you saying, "Hey, we didn't want a sermon, just an update." Well, don't complain. At least I'm not asking for an offering! Remember, I am a trained, ordained, Free Lutheran pastor. Don't be fooled by the word, 'Free'. We have ways of making you pay. Don't tempt me.

The last two weeks of hospice care have had their ups and downs. Pain control has been excellent, thanks be to God. Appetite, digestion, strength, and sleep have had some big swings. Considering how sick Jeannie is, I believe things are going as good as we could expect. Jeannie has been able to lessen the amount of meds she takes. This has enabled her to function better. She is very weak. She becomes fatigued easily. It frustrates her a little.

However, the last two Sundays she has been able to attend one of our three morning worship services. I told Kayla that I saw Jeannie nod off during my message. Kayla said, "You don't need to be concerned about that, Dad. She even did that before she was sick." For you that don't know who Kayla is, she is our third daughter who used to be in our Will.

God has surrounded us with great caregivers. Our daughters, extended family, nurse co-workers, and a faithful church family have all enfolded us with love. Added to this, is the wonderful care of our hospice nurse and home health care givers. If that wasn't enough, God has encircled us with a global network of praying friends in Christ. We are blessed beyond measure.

Let me share with you one final and very personal thought. Jeannie told me yesterday, that she felt somewhat purposeless. I said to her, "Really, explain that to me." Then she enumerated all the things she hasn't had the strength or ability to do. She said, "I just sit, try to eat, fall asleep when I shouldn't, and can't sleep, when I should." I responded, "You mean you'd like to do all these things we are doing for you?" She nodded with a yes. After a few moments, I shared my heart with her. "Jeannie, even though I believe I know what you mean, I want you to understand something from my point of view. I appreciate all that you've done for me during our marriage, but your greatest purpose in my life is just in your 'being'. I can hire someone to cook or clean or iron, but only you can be you. I praise God for each moment you and I can just 'be'. It goes way beyond anything you can do or say or any intimacy of our flesh. It is an intimacy of our being made one. And this purpose far out weighs them all. Only you are one with me."

One day Jeannie's 'being' on earth will come to an end. So will mine and so will yours. If Jeannie's comes before mine, only God will be able to fill the void. And He will.

Until then, I will rejoice in every day of purpose He has meant for us as husband and wife. If you are married, I hope you'll think about this. Don't let any other good purpose of daily tasks in life, steal away God's best purpose of oneness in spirit.

Strongly Woven As A Three Strand Cord,
Jeannie, Me, and Jesus

Chapter Eighteen: A Bad Night...

Kayla Brandt

Dad and I cared for Mom every evening when I got off work. We had good nights and bad. Some nights were wrought with physical complications. One night was especially bad. It was the night following the first day Mom received chemo. Although the chemo treatment itself had gone well, the next day told an entirely different story. Alisha met the morning head-on with the onslaught of vomiting. It continued every half hour throughout the day. I had been out of town and was flying home that afternoon. I talked to Alisha briefly that morning and knew that Mom was starting to slide downhill. I wouldn't know how far she had slid until later that evening. No sooner had my plane hit the ground than my phone began to ring.

It was a Wednesday night and Dad needed to go to church for Bible study. I arrived at the house to find it dimly lit and Dad standing at the top of the stairs. He was pacing and humming, a signal that we had quickly learned meant he was nervous. He whispered to me about the chemo treatment, how Mom reacted, that she was resting in bed, and indicated the medications she had been sent home with to ease the poisoning effects of chemo. Cupped in his hands, Dad held several bottles of pills and explained to me when each one was to be given and what they were supposed to help with. But the drugs weren't helping. Dad held them out to me in his hands and cried out in frustration, "They're not working!" He didn't know what to do. I stood there staring at him. I had honestly never seen my Dad shaken. But he stood now in front me almost like a child, desperate and hopeless because his wife was hurting.

Our conversation came to an abrupt halt when Mom stirred in the bedroom and quickly made her way to the bathroom for another round of vomiting. Dad went in to help her. I ran downstairs to the other bathroom to vomit myself. It was a sympathetic reaction to the sight and sound of my mother's pain. I gathered myself, shook it off and went back upstairs. Dad figured out what had happened and, I think, was scared to leave me there with Mom. I assured him that it was out of my system and that I was just unprepared for how bad it had become almost over night. Dad left and Mom and I laid together on her bed. She was dehydrated, lethargic and wiped out. I was tired from traveling. So we laid there together, enfolded in the warmth of her down comforter, mother and daughter.

From: Pastor Michael Brandt <pastorbrandt@knowingthesavior.org>
To: Family and Friends in Christ
Subject Jeannie Update 5/9/05

May 9, 2005,

Dear Family and Friends in Christ,

"Charm is deceitful and beauty is vain, but a woman who fears the Lord, she shall be praised," Proverbs 31:30.

There is nothing quite so beautiful as the reflection of Christ in the face of a mother. Jeannie has been mothering for 33 years. If you count the time she has had to 'mother' me, it would be 36! This day, I would join my daughters in rising up, to honor God and bless Jeannie! All the years of our time together, especially in these last days, she has beautifully mirrored the image of Jesus. Even in the midst of her trials, she praises God by the strength He provides. What an encouragement and witness of honoring and fearing the Lord, she is to me and her family.

I have not written for quite a while. The changes we have seen lately have been gradual. Pain control has continued to go well, but some of the pain meds, taken orally, upset Jeannie's stomach. Next week they are going to increase the dosage in the pain patches by 50%. This will lessen the amount of narcotics she will need to swallow. PTL!

Jeannie is very weak. She doesn't eat much. She sleeps a great deal of the time. However, her mind is sharp and her spirit is at peace. Each night we read the Word and pray. Because it is hard for her to speak, I do the 'out loud' praying. At the end, I hear her sweet, soft voice declare, "I love you Jesus!" She does. I do. Because He first loved us.

Someone asked me, "What do you do when you are waiting to die?" The answer came quickly, "If you are trusting in Christ, you LIVE!" It really is that simple. In fact, all of us are either in the process of dying or waiting for Jesus' 2nd Coming. You do believe He is coming again, don't you? If you don't, you really should not celebrate Christmas. Why? Because the same Bible that told us of Jesus' 1st Coming, tells us the Risen Christ is coming again. Did you know that there are more prophecies in the Bible concerning Christ's 2nd Coming, than His 1st Coming? When you consider that the prophecies dealing with His 1st Coming were all fulfilled with precision, shouldn't you take the prophecies concerning His 2nd Coming seriously? Hopefully, you do. Jeannie and I do. Therefore, we have hope and peace in the face of death. While we wait, we LIVE! We live victoriously. We grieve with hope and we joyously anticipate seeing Jesus face to face. Now, that is LIVING! Here is the Good News, "For God so loved the world, that WHOSOEVER believes in Him, shall not perish, but shall have everlasting LIFE!"

Both Jeannie and I want you to wait to die, in the same way we are; resting in the everlasting arms of the Lord of Life.

Safe and Secure in the Arms of Jesus,
Jeannie and Michael

Chapter Nineteen: Sunday Morning Worship...

Kayla Brandt

Other nights were better and we enjoyed the simple pleasure of just being together. I had the blessing of participating in nightly devotions with my parents. We read the Psalms, and I watched as my mother gained God's peace and comfort through His Word. Her ears loved to hear it. We prayed together. We gave thanks for the strength that God was providing, and we pleaded for His continued mercy and grace. Our nights created memories to hold onto, but the time I treasured most was Sunday mornings with Mom.

Because I was single and did not have a family, I was granted unprecedented permission from Dad to skip church on Sunday mornings to take care of Mom. They were quiet hours while Dad and the rest of the girls were at church. Sunday mornings became privileged, private moments that I looked forward to. Mom would still be sleeping when I arrived, and I would ever so gently push open the bedroom door, sit across from her bed and watch her. I was trying to memorize her. But no matter how quiet I was, she would hear me. With the door eased open and the curtains raised, Mom would wake from her slumber, crack open her eyes and smile at me.

Come to think of it, all of our lives Mom's ears heard everything. Whether it was squabbling and fighting or a cry in the middle of the night, no sound from her girls escaped Mom's ears. On the down side, sometimes this meant being spanked. On the up side, sometimes this meant being rescued.

Climbing out of bed was always a process for Mom. Her body had to adjust to the shock of moving again. When she was ready to face the day, we took it one arm and one leg at a time. Once Mom was sitting upright on the edge of the bed, she wrapped her arms around my neck, and I wrapped my arms around her waist. Together, we rose up and stood in one swift motion. And then she held me there in that embrace. I like to pretend that I was holding her, but, really, Mom was holding me. We whispered, "I love you," in each others' ears and began God's day. It was our worship service, and it was sacred.

From: Pastor Michael Brandt <pastorbrandt@knowingthesavior.org>
To: Family and Friends in Christ
Subject: Jeannie Update 5/16/05

May 16, 2005,

Dear Family and Friends in Christ,

"Even though I walk through the valley of the shadow of death, I fear no evil; for Thou art with me; Thy rod and Thy staff, they comfort me," Psalm 23:4.

Jeannie is walking deeper into this valley day by day.

Jesus has already passed through this valley. He is walking with Jeannie right now. In fact, He is carrying her. He is carrying us (the girls and me) too.

This past week, we ordered a hospital bed. It was just too much for her to walk back and forth to our bedroom and the bathroom. We are trying to meet all of Jeannie's bodily needs in a way that will allow her to conserve energy. Her appetite is nonexistent. It is even hard to swallow water. Ice chips are a blessing. Jello is a treat. The swelling in her feet and legs is increasing. Her breathing is shallow. Her mind is sharp. Her spirit is sweet and calm, as she waits for Christ's call.

The valley is dark. It is deep. BUT ... the Light of Christ dispels the darkness AND the Grace of God is deeper than the valley. Jeannie fears no evil, for her Savior is with her, right inside her. He's already been through this valley of death. HE CONQUERED IT! His presence is our peace.

In the midst of the journey, we sense His loving hand. When we become nervous, His staff pulls us towards Him. When we hesitate, His rod gently prods us step by step on this previously unknown path. His acts of compassion and loving kindness never cease. Our Shepherd is GOOD!

The girls and I are being given strength too. We talk and we pray. Ready for Jeannie's death? Yes and no. But we are confident ... confident of God's love and grace ... confident of Jeannie's testimony ... confident of God's and each other's love ... confident of Christ's promises and the Spirit's comfort ... confident of the Heavenly home Jesus has prepared for those who lovingly have surrendered to Him. God is ready and He's the One we are trusting.

Thanks for praying in Jesus' Name for us. He hears and He answers. His answers are always best. His will is always right. His ways are beyond questioning, for His love is beyond any measure known to man. We love you, Jesus.

Walking in the Light of His Presence,
Jeannie and Michael

Chapter Twenty: Beauty in Death...

Kayla Brandt

Is there beauty in death? For believers there is. We can only imagine the glory and splendor of Heaven. We have the visions of the Apostle John about streets paved with gold, the throne of God framed in a gleaming emerald rainbow, and crystal seas of life. John goes on to describe the brilliance and magnificence of the sights of Heaven and the resounding echoes of choirs of angels singing. All of this majestic detail is given to us in the Scriptures, and it was merely a glimpse. John saw just a brief glimpse.

Our human minds cannot even begin to capture in our imaginations the pure glory of what awaits us in God's kingdom. Our mother is there. She is perfect. She has no pain and no sorrow. She has been greeted and welcomed into her Father's embrace and is His good and faithful servant finally home. She has bowed down at the holy feet of God. Her beautiful voice is singing praises to her Savior. She is dancing at the throne.

Yes, there is beauty in death if one has claimed the promise that God gives his children. Isaiah 49:15-16 says, "I will not forget you. See I have engraved you here in the palms of My hands." It is a promise. A promise fulfilled for our Mother.

From: Bill Mitchell <bmitchell@knowingthesavior.org>
To: Family and Friends in Christ
Subject: Jeannie Update 5/22/05

May 22, 2005,

Please pray for Pastor Mike and his family as Jeannie went home to be with our Lord at about 1:30 this afternoon. Pray for God's peace, comfort and strength for the entire family.

"The Lord makes me very happy; all that I am rejoices in my God. He has covered me with clothes of salvation and wrapped me with a coat of goodness" Isaiah 61:10

Chapter Twenty-one: Our Last Sunday Morning...

Kayla Brandt

M om passed away on a Sunday. The Saturday before brought many signs and signals that the end was drawing near. God was still in control and continued to give us grace. He again brought Ona and Benjy into town that weekend. And Mom's parents were driven down from the cities that day to see their daughter one last time. Poor little Isabelle and Wesley had only been allowed to see Gramma for short periods of time over the previous couple of weeks. It was hard to explain to toddlers that they had to be quiet and gentle and couldn't attack and smother Gramma Jeannie with hugs and kisses.

On that Saturday, Mom drifted in and out of slumber and consciousness. Isabelle and Wesley were brought to visit. We held them over Mom to lean in and kiss her tenderly on the cheek. When they were ready to leave, the two toddlers stood at the end of Mom's bed and exclaimed, "Bye, Gramma Jeannie! Love you, Gramma Jeannie!" Their little hands waved fast and furious. Suddenly Mom sat straight up, smiled, and waved fast and furious back to them. It was a precious moment of clarity. It was a God thing.

That Saturday night all four of us girls and Dad gathered around Mom's bed. We encircled her. We drew in together again like we had the very first night of Mom's illness. We steadied each other and kept one another from falling. We rose up and called Mom blessed. We told Mom that we loved her. She was aware that we were all there and said I love you back to each of us. It is a vivid memory forever etched on our hearts.

Sunday morning came and we knew without a doubt that Mom would very soon be going home. Ona and Benjy planned on taking care of Mom that morning so I could attend church. I called to check on them when I woke up to make sure they were doing okay and heard Ona's tears on the other end of the phone. I panicked.

"What's wrong, Ona?" I probed. It had been a few weeks since they had provided the caregiving, and I was worried that they were having a problem.

"Mom's getting worse," she choked out. She could hardly speak between the cries she was trying to stifle.

"What is happening?" I kept asking. I was worried now, concerned about Mom and the two of them. I didn't want them to be alone when Mom passed away. I jumped back into the role of the strong one. I kept asking questions trying to gain an understanding of how bad it was and why she was so upset, but Ona could hardly answer me.

"She's just getting worse, Kayla," she said again. "Have you called Dad?" I asked. I thought that Dad was at church and knew he would need to come home. He would be able to get there quicker than I could.

"He didn't go," Ona sighed. Relief washed over me. Dad was there. It somehow made everything better.

I rushed over to the house and went straight up the stairs. Mom was breathing. She was still with us. I silently whispered thanks to God for enabling me to make it there before she died. I leaned in close to Mom's face, kissed her cheek, and told her that I loved her one last time.

Alisha, Erika and their families had gone to church that morning before we were able to reach them on the phone, but they grasped by Dad's absence in the pulpit that Mom's time was near. Again, God delivered grace. They both left the service and hastened to the house. Isaac and Emma touched Gramma Jeannie's hand, kissed her, expressed their "I love yous." Alisha knelt down next to Mom's bed like she had in the beginning. She softly caressed Mom's brow, and kissed her while tears streamed down her face. Sherwin dropped off Erika, and left to take Isabelle and Wesley to his parents' house. Erika, too, knelt down next to Mom, grasped her hand, gazed upon her and said, "I love you," just as she had the very first night. Darryl and Benjy placed coats on Isaac and Emma, deciding to go to the grocery store to get us something to eat.

And so there we were – our beloved mother, Dad, and the four daughters. Tragedy drew us together like it had in the beginning. We asked for and graciously received one final moment of privacy. God granted us another measure of grace. At about 1:30 p.m. Mom slipped in and sighed out her last breath. Jeannie's Michael and Jeannie's girls huddled together and gathered around the one they loved. Tears streamed down our faces, we gasped in our next breath, we grieved, and we comforted each other.

Soon, the rest of the family returned home. The kids cried, but were not afraid. They needed assurance from the adults that this was "just Gramma Jeannie's earthly body, right? Her spirit and soul are in Heaven with Jesus?" They were correct. They understood. We gave validation and with it came comfort and peace for the little ones. We sat there as a family together and cried. We read the promises of Scripture. We prayed. We breathed in the comfort that the Holy Spirit washed over us. When we were ready to part with Mom's earthly remains, the hospice nurse and funeral home were called. Phone calls to extended family started to be dialed. Family members began to arrive. Soon, the house was filled again with the commotion of life. We talked. We laughed. We cried. We remembered. We held onto each other and lifted one another up.

From: Pastor Michael Brandt <pastorbrandt@knowingthesavior.org>
To: Family and Friends in Christ
Subject: Jeannie Update 5/23/05

May 23, 2005,

Dear Family and Friends in Christ,

"Precious in the sight of the Lord is the death of His Godly ones (saints)," Psalm 116:15.

From my earthly point of view, this is one update I have dreaded writing. Yet, from Heaven's perspective, it is the most glorious news anyone could ever hope to proclaim. Yes, like Lazarus, Jeannie Marie has been taken up by the angels into the very bosom of her Heavenly Father. My earthly loss is Heaven's precious Home Coming. The very Home Coming Jeannie so long for, especially in these last days. As Cyndi (a coworker of Jeannie's) said, "It's not an untimely death. From Heaven's account, she is safely Home and right on time!" With tears of joy and sadness, I agree.

Am I speaking arrogantly, to call Jeannie a saint? Not at all. Jeannie was a saint, not by natural birth or by her good works, which were many, but by the grace of Jesus, she experienced a spiritual birth. Abandoning all of her own works of righteousness, she cried out to Jesus, "Lord, have mercy on me, a sinner!" By the amazing grace of God in Christ, His blood washed her white as snow. In childlike faith she asked, "Jesus, come into my heart today, come in to stay." By faith, she was made new by His indwelling presence. Take a moment to read the words of Jesus in John 17:23-26. Jesus longs to make saints out of all broken sinners, who will call upon Him for salvation.

Jeannie's last days were ones of rapid decline. The hospital bed was a blessing, but it was also a clear indication of the cancer's increasing effects. Thankfully, her caregivers and her daily meds enabled good pain control. By Wednesday of this past week, Jeannie and I could see the end was very near. Our children, plus Jeannie's parents were able to be by her side. Wonderful memories, precious Scripture readings, marvelous hymns, along with laughter and tears filled our moments. Saturday afternoon, her mom and dad left for Bloomington knowing the end was near. By Saturday evening, the girls and I discussed the need for me to surrender my pulpit privileges to Pastor Mark Chase. He willingly accepted.

Sunday morning awakened us to the reality that Heaven's angels were ready to take Jeannie Home. She called out my name and then slipped into a series of sighs. Upon our call, the hospice nurse came and assured us that the end was indeed near and that, to the best of her assessment, Jeannie was not in any unusual pain. With each breath, death drew nearer. At 1:30 pm, Jeannie arrived safely at Home in Heaven and breathed in all of eternity! Oh, how her soul must have burst, as she cried out, "Lord Jesus, I love you!" And how her spirit must have tingled as He said, "Welcome, My good and faithful daughter!"

How could I ever want anything less for her? My dear Jeannie Marie is safely Home. Yes, right on time!

As of this writing, the specific day and time of Jeannie's Celebration of Life Service has not been set. We will be meeting with the funeral home staff tomorrow. I will send out another e-mail after that meeting. In the meantime, please know how grateful I am for your faithful prayer support.

One At Home and One On the Way,
Jeannie & Michael

Chapter Twenty-two: "Did You See Him?"

Kayla Brandt

Evening fell quickly upon us the night Mom died, and soon it was time for Alisha and Darryl to gather Isaac and Emma and head home. They all said their goodbyes and packed up into the truck. Alisha was exhausted. She was emotionally drained and sat in reflective silence. Thoughts raced through her head. She wanted to get home. Alisha needed to cry hard in private. Emma had been playing outside and was still fairly wound up. She chattered non-stop as usual. Her round face, blonde tousled hair, rosy cheeks, and bright blue eyes raced with life. Alisha tuned her out. It was a skill she had acquired along the way with Emma. Emma never stops talking. Even if you exit the room and return, she is still talking to you and has been the entire time you were gone. The rest of us girls think Emma is delightful and hilarious. Alisha does, too, she just tunes her out once in a while for the sake of sanity. But Emma would not be ignored that night.

"Mom," her low gruff voice called out from the back seat.

"What Emma," Alisha responded.

"Did you see him?" Emma asked.

"See who, Emma?" Alisha probed back.

"Did you see him?" Emma asked again.

Alisha drifted back to her own thoughts and didn't respond this time.

From the backseat the question came again. "Did you see him?"

There was a little more persistence this time from Emma and Alisha did reply, "Did I see who, Emma?" Alisha was becoming frustrated with Emma's continuing probing. Whatever Emma was getting at didn't seem all that important. But it was. Emma was frustrated too.

She didn't understand why her mom didn't get it, and raised her voice this time and asked again with force, "Did you see him?"

"Who, Emma?!" Alisha exclaimed back.

"*Jesus*, Mom!" Emma shouted. "Did you see Jesus when he came to get Gramma?"

And then it was clear. It was exactly what the children were told all along since Mom became ill. Gramma Jeannie was very sick and Jesus would come soon to take her to Heaven. Emma remembered. She understood with perfect child-like faith and innocence that when you died, Jesus came to get you.

And Emma was upset. She had claimed her Gramma Jeannie's Jesus. He was in her heart. She was excited to see Him. Emma just couldn't believe it. She was a little irritated that during their short trip to the grocery store she had missed her chance to see Jesus come to get her Gramma. She wanted to meet Him, literally. She thought she missed seeing it all happen. Oh, that we were all waiting anxiously to meet Jesus like Emma is! Is there beauty in death? Out of the precious mouths of babes in childlike faith, yes, there is beauty in death.

From: Pastor Michael Brandt <pastorbrandt@knowingthesavior.org>
To: Family and Friends in Christ
Subject: Jeannie Update 5/24/05

May 24, 2005,

Dear Family and Friends in Christ,

"This is the day the Lord has made, I WILL rejoice and be glad in it," Psalm 118:24.

When we consider the gift of Jesus, we have all the reason in the world to rejoice. Added to that, we have the gift He gave us in Jeannie. This is a day for us to treasure her memory.

O the wonder of it all. On this day, when we have a visitation service of praise and prayer, let me pay tribute to the God of her creation and redemption, by remembering the earthly life, gifts, and talents He entrusted to her.

The wonder of Jeannie is impossible for me to adequately describe. An amazing wife, mother, grandmother, daughter, sister, and friend.

Her eyes were beautiful and her focus was sharp. They expressed the very love of heart and the zest of her spirit. They focused on Jesus and His Word, and because of that you knew she focused on you too. The look of loving care and genuine concern radiated from her eyes. How grateful I am to have had them cast the look of love on me.

Her ears were beautiful too. From the notes of a bell choir to the silent cry of a hurting heart, Jeannie had a keen sense of hearing. She always had time to listen, first to God, but also to us. She really did listen, more than words, she listened to you. Without a doubt, her ears were directly connected to her heart. How grateful I am to have had them finely tuned to hear every sound of my life.

Her mouth and lips were spectacular. Songs of worship and words of praise flowed from her lips unto God. Always ready to give a reason for the hope of her salvation. Always eager to give a word of encouragement. And for a select few: husband, daughters, grandkids, parents, and a few close relatives and friends, her lips gave us the sweet kiss of love. How grateful I am to have heard and tasted her loving lips.

Her arms and hands were long and tender. Long enough to enfold you in a sincere embrace and long enough to reach around any task. Gentle to the touch, yet strong in her grip (she never dropped a handbell). Quick to give a hand of help or pat of approval. Even in discipline, they were lovingly applied. Faithfully out stretched and open for God to use. Lifted in praise and folded in prayer, her arms and her hands were beautiful. Especially one hand, that by God's grace she entrusted to me in marriage.

Her knees were well worn. Repentfully bent in confession of sin and in respectful honor of her Savior. Kindly bent in submission to any task.

Tenderly bent to better care for a child. Dutifully bent in lowly tasks, that she considered a high privilege. O, how beautiful Jeannie's knees were. How grateful I am that she knelt before the altar of God with me and knelt in prayerfor me.

Her legs and feet carried her well. Legs that carried her elegantly striding by faith on the paths of righteousness God set before her. Feet that did not stray from the path of God's Word. Legs and feet, that hastily stepped up to any call of service. Beautiful feet shod with the Gospel of peace. Footprints, we would do well to follow. How grateful I am to have had the privilege of walking through 40 years of life together (36 as husband and wife).

Her heart was most beautiful of all. In the midst of this serious tribute, I must say, "I know Jeannie was not perfect. On one occasion, I witnessed her doing a rolling stop at a stop sign. It was not a complete stop." Yet, her heart was covered by the blood of Calvary. A heart which honestly confessed its sinfulness. A heart that opened to welcome Jesus to come in, to come in to stay. A heart longing to be filled by the Spirit, day by day. A heart beating with the very compassion of Heaven. A heart, by the grace of God, poured out for Christ, for you, and might I say from personal experience, for me. A heart filled with eternity's hope, a hope now fully realized. Yes, a heart peacefully at rest, yet pounding with an exhilaration none of us can fully comprehend. How grateful, I am to have had my heart united with hers until death us did part.

In thanks to God and in honor of His creation, Jeannie Marie, I give this inadequate tribute. If she were here, she would cringe. However, she is not here. It is not being done for her. It is being done so I will never forget how I am to live my life. It is being done for the glory due Her Creator and Redeemer. He is not cringing, for He is the One who said to her on Sunday, "Well done Thou good and faithful servant, enter into the joy of My and your Rest."

In Honor of A Life Well Lived and Praise God, Lived With Me,
Michael

OBITUARY
Jeanne M. Brandt
January 22, 1947 - May 22, 2005

JEANNE M. BRANDT- 1201 N. Connor Trail, Sioux Falls, SD; Died: Sunday, May 22, 2005, Sioux Falls, SD; Age: 58 years, 4 months

PRAISE AND PRAYER SERVICE- 7:00 PM Tuesday, May 24, 2005, Abiding Savior Free Lutheran Church, Sioux Falls, SD; Reverend Elden Nelson, Officiating, Jodi Marcum, Accompanist, "He Will Carry Me" - Darin Dykstra, Vocalist, "Somebody's Praying Me Through" - Darrell Schmith, Vocalist, Congregational Hymn - Jay Marcum, Hymn Leader, "'Tis So Sweet to Trust in Jesus'"

CELEBRATION OF LIFE SERVICE- 1:00 PM Wednesday, May 25, 2005, Abiding Savior Free Lutheran Church, Sioux Falls, SD; Reverend Elden Nelson, Service Leader, Reverend Jim Johnson (Jeanne's Brother), Word of Tribute and Thanks to God, Reverend Robert Lee, Message, Jodi Marcum, Accompanist - Louisa Biteler, Violinist, Praise Music - Abiding Savior Praise Team, "Trusting You Alone" - Eric Dubs, Vocalist, Congregational Hymns - Jay Marcum, Hymn Leader, "Be Thou My Vision", "Great is Thy Faithfulness"

INTERMENT- Splitrock Lutheran Cemetery, Rural Brandon, SD

PALLBEARERS- Samuel Goodhope, Greg Breukelman, Micah Stevenson, Brandt Stevenson, Zachary Johnson, Travis Johnson

HONORARY PALLBEARERS- Ben Johnson, Seth Johnson, Isaiah Johnson, Titus Johnson

Jeanne Marie Johnson, daughter of Lyell and Lois Johnson, was born January 22, 1947 in Minneapolis, MN. She was raised in Bloomington, MN and graduated from Bloomington High School in 1964. She graduated from California Lutheran Bible School, Los Angeles, CA with a degree in Biblical studies in 1966. Jeanne earned a Bachelor of Science Degree in

Nursing in 1970 from St. Olaf College, Northfield, MN. For the past 13 years she has been privileged to give nursing care at the Sioux Falls Surgical Center.

Jeanne was united in marriage with Reverend Michael Brandt on April 5, 1969 in Bloomington, MN. They were blessed with four daughters. Jeanne and Michael served congregations in Lake Stevens, WA, Amery, WI and Cloquet, MN before moving to Sioux Falls, SD where they are currently serving at Abiding Savior Free Lutheran Church. In everything from music to nursery child care, Jeanne loved serving Christ and people.

Grateful for having shared her life are her husband, Michael; four daughters, Erika DeWitt and her husband, Sherwin, Brandon, SD, Alisha Nelson and her husband, Darryl, Garretson, SD, Kayla Brandt, Sioux Falls, SD, Ona Deubner and her husband, Benjamin, Grand Forks, ND; five grandchildren, Isaac and Emma Nelson, Isabelle, Wesley and Baby DeWitt; her parents, Lyell and Lois Johnson, Bloomington, MN; one sister, Lori Alsdurf, Maplewood, MN; two brothers, Kim Johnson and his wife, Cathy, Eagan, MN, Reverend James Johnson and his wife, Linda, Plymouth, MN; and a host of other relatives and friends.

Relatives and friends are invited to gather with the family for refreshments and fellowship at Abiding Savior Free Lutheran Church following the Celebration of Life service and prior to leaving for the committal service.

In lieu of flowers, Jeanne's family requests that memorials be directed to the Legacy of Faith Foundation at Abiding Savior Free Lutheran Church.

JEANNE'S THEME VERSE

Thy words were found, and I did eat them; and Thy Word was unto me the joy and rejoicing of mine heart: for I am called by Thy name, O Lord God of Hosts.

Jeremiah 15:16

Jeanne: Wiping the Kisses From My Cheek

By James L. Johnson
May 25, 2005
Jeanne's Funeral, Sioux Falls, South Dakota

Do you think God sends us people like this? God sends a prophet, an evangelist, a shepherd, an elegant Mom, a real gramma, a daughter and sister and wife from the Lord, an unforgettable soprano, alternating verses with that unique female tenor, one octave higher, with a heart for the truth? Don't you think God brings messengers: a nurse, a witness, a vibrant Christian lady who shows you how to follow Jesus Christ? That's what happened to me, anyway.

I thank the Lord for sending people like that. Jesus lives in them.

I watched that Jesus up close in Jeanne and Michael Brandt for years. Jeanne let me live with her family for five summers – they were the months I gave my life to Christ. I learned to let Him be my Lord. She was the one who talked me into going to Bible school. I learned to do youth ministry at their church in Wisconsin. Erika, Alisha, Kayla and Ona became little sisters and Michael became a mentor and friend.

Looking back, I have to confess: It wasn't Jeanne who changed me, or Michael, or the four Brandt girls – or even people like you. But the Holy Spirit began speaking to the heart of a teenage boy and college student she called her baby brother. She squeezed my left cheek as if she owned it. In so many ways, the woman I fell in love with at age 22, my sweet Linda, was a 1980s version of Jeanne, without the soprano-tenor combination. Linda was a young Bible student who was teaching VBS at Jeanne's church in

1984. Jeanne and Mike were impressed, too: "If you don't ask her out," Mike said. "I'll ask her out for you."

We've been married for 18 years now.

Now each hymn or worship song, each four-part harmony, every plate of scrambled eggs, makes me think of one of the most influential Christians I ever met. How much I owe her. But how much more I owe the God she and Michael helped expose me to. I met Jeanne Brandt when her name was Jeanne Johnson. We attended the same church, were raised in the same home, loved the same brother and sister, Kim and Lori, adored the same parents, Lois and Lyell. Mom named her Jeanne, one syllable, two "n"s. People couldn't help but add the "ie." To Dad and Mom and the rest of us, that beaming strawberry blond became "Jeannie." She grew up in a south Minneapolis suburb with 10,000 other kids who moved into its new ramblers, cement driveways, tar and pebble avenues running north and south, east and west. But she was different than the rest.

The first time I ever laid eyes on her was when she was a sophomore. She was 15; I was one week old. Dad pulled her out of school so she could hold me on the way home from Swedish Hospital. He laid me on two pillows on Jeanne's knees for the ride home to our rambler by the airport. I've been resting in her lap, so to speak, ever since. It's the same for a lot of you, I suppose.

God took care of us, using people like that.

During the last four decades, Mike and Jeanne were a team, bringing a simple message: Jesus Christ died on a cross and rose from the dead. He lives and grants forgiveness to all who repent. They planted churches, raised four daughters, spoke to you, lived with you, prayed for you, starting churches with 25 or 30 or 50 and praying them to, well, what you see here today. Mike has a gift for evangelism; Jeannie the gift for discernment. He wins souls, she helped them grow. They raised their family among people like you and let you in on their lives. They let you sit on their lap.

That's the way God used them for me, anyway. My doting parents, Lois and Lyell, remain ever close, but Jeanne and Mike were always surrogates. Mom and Dad asked her to be my godmother. I was as much their little boy as their baby brother – and now I serve Jesus as a pastor, as they have served Him.

Of all the qualities that I have loved in the years since, the most significant are three: the voice, the look, and the Savior.

First, the voice. Can't you hear it? Jeanne sang even when she spoke, with a spiritual rhythm that carried a lilt and laughter, with a pace and pulse that gave it poetry, power and prose. When she sang, she carried you into the ether with a versatile woman's voice that soared to soprano or tunneled to tenor, high or low, like a Lutheran Julie Andrews. The hills came alive with her sounds of music. Especially when she sang about Jesus. Raindrops on roses are nothing compared to the brown paper packages she tied with string. The Holy Spirit tied you up when the Lutheran pastor's wife, perpetual mother, a youngish grandma, and particular nurse sang about the Savior. Jeanne sang "Jesus Never Fails" on my wedding day and left me blind and bawling, my face contorted with tears, through three-fourths of the ceremony.

How many people get a voice like that?

Equally significant about Jeanne was the look. When she asked you how you were doing, there was something about her face that made you want to tell the truth. She could read it on your face. My mother Lois said that ever since Jeanne was two years old, she always could hear more, could see more, could cut to the quick before almost anyone else. "She always knew more than me," said Mom. We all believe it was the presence of the Holy Spirit. God lived in her and we saw His glory, glory as of the only begotten of the Father, full of grace and truth. One day when I was 11, we dropped Jeanne off at the airport, to rejoin Michael in ministry in Washington. When she saw me again before stepping out to leave, she turned around and gave me that look. It was something about her eyebrows and cheeks, the quick embrace, the thoughtful gaze. But I found myself looking at the God that was living in her. Eleven year old boys don't cry a lot. But I cried then and I cry now, at 43, because I came to know that God.

The look was a powerful tool from God. She could use it in many ways, like when Linda and I visited 22 days ago and she asked where the baby was. "Sleeping in the car," I said. She gave me the look, and two penetrating words: "All alone," she said. I knew what she wanted. I fetched the baby. In a larger sense, I suppose, that's how we all feel right now. "All alone." We miss that voice and we miss that look. But we are not alone. We don't have the voice and we don't have the look, but we have the Jesus. James 4:13-14 says that we are vapors, "Come now, you who say, 'Today or tomorrow we will go to such and such a city, and spend a year there and engage in business and make a profit.' Yet you do not know what your life will be like tomorrow," says James 3. "You are just a vapor that appears for a little while and then vanishes away. Instead, you ought to say, 'If the Lord wills, we will do this or that.'"

Jesus is not a vapor. Jeanne was vapor, you and I are vapors. But God does not appear for a little while and vanish away. He is solid and steady and firm and still here. That's what Jeanne told me, and I believe it because it's true.

The apostle John never mentioned his own name in his gospel. He called himself, "the one whom Jesus loved." I feel the same way. I'm the boy whom Jeanne loved. I'm an ordained pastor, father of nine, leader of a Bible school. But way down deep, I'm only two things: a disciple of Jesus Christ, and, like you, someone whom Jeanne loved.

And didn't she love the children the most?

When she would visit our house, Jeanne always greeted us each by name, even the nine children, having memorized each name and face, giving them the look, using that voice. And then she would come to me: "How's my baby brother?" she would ask.

When she would say such a thought, my mind would wander to my childhood, saying goodbye at the door of our parents' house in East Bloomington. When Jeanne used to kiss me on the cheek with her ruby red lipstick, my chubby little hand could not resist the urge to dry my face immediately. Each time her eyes wilted. She gave me that look and sang in that voice: "Don't wipe it off!" Her droopy eyes made me strangely sorry for such an insult. You don't wipe kisses off when they come from a woman like that.

Watching Jeanne and Mike, I learned to love kids, to adore little girls, to discipline children, to sing to kids, to laugh with them, to treasure kids. She solidified the values my amazing mother impressed on me. When a big sister repeats what a great mother teaches, a chubby little blond guy can hardly disagree. Even if he wipes off their kisses. With those kinds of gifts and that level of character, any slip from perfection was always a historical event with Jeanne. During a weak moment, she once called her six-year-old Alisha, in consecutive order, a "pea-brain" and a "bird brain" while I sat at the kitchen table with Mike and Erika and Kayla at the table. Baby Ona was in the high chair. We were honored to be present. "Since when do we call our children 'pea brain?'" Michael asked. Somehow it was refreshing to know that Jeanne was one of us. Jeanne smiled and apologized, caught in her sin. One rolling stop, as Michael described last night, and one moment calling her beloved child a pea brain. That's not much for which to account. But we knew it was a day to remember. I bet you are jealous that you never saw it happen. But I saw it and I learned.

I learned from Jeanne that we are all sinners. And vapors, too... And even the best of us. Even Jeanne. We baby boomers have been suckled to believe that we are forever young. We take to heart the promise of Psalm 90, that life is "seventy years, or if due to strength, eighty." We think God owes us that much. But He does not owe us. Jesus never promises a tomorrow. Jeanne and Mike used to tell me that as a teenager who was as yet not sold out for Christ. He gives you today, so don't wait until tomorrow. He died on the cross back then so you could accept His forgiveness today.

Why won't you receive the Jesus Christ that Jeanne followed?

Today I thank the Lord for that God, that Jesus, and that lady. I'm thinking about how rapidly life changes, how real heaven is and how grateful I am for that tenth grade girl who held me on pillows on the way home from Swedish Hospital. When I feel like I'm alone, I'll remember that voice, think about that look, and turn to that Savior.

One day I will die. So will you. Until then, I figure, I'll live my life for Jesus, like many want to do. I'll serve Him to the end – and prepare for the day when I vanish away and go to heaven and attend the Wedding Feast of the Lamb.

With Jeanne.

I hope, when I'm there, that I can hear the Julie Andrews of the Free Lutherans sing the sounds of music again. I'll listen to her sing worship songs to the Lord.

If she kisses me on the cheek that day, I'll try not to wipe it off.

Chapter Twenty-three: Do We Miss Her?

Kayla Brandt

Do we miss her? Miss is an understatement. Does she miss us? Isabelle peered up out of her cereal bowl one morning, "Mom, Gramma really misses us."

"She does?" Erika questioned, puzzled by her daughter's comment.

"Yes, she does," Isabelle continued, "And she told God the other day, 'God, I really miss my family,' but then God told her, 'Don't worry. Pretty soon they are going to die and come up here anyway.'"

It's hard to explain to a lonely five-year-old that Gramma really doesn't miss us. She can't. Heaven contains no sorrow. No pain. No sadness. But I can say with certainty that we do miss Mom even though she isn't missing us.

Mom loved life and she loved Jesus. He was her first love. Her second love was her family. She gave of herself constantly as a wife, mother, and grandmother. Many words portray the essence of Mom – joy, mercy, strength, hope, light, love, grace. I could write a book containing just words depicting the amazement of Mom. However, she was perhaps best described in two words – Gramma Jeannie. Mom was anxious to be a grandma. She loved children. She had looked forward to the opportunity to be a grandma, and she considered it a privilege. There is no question that she was an amazing one. She was the kind of grandma that little legs scurried to with open arms so she could embrace you, lift you up in her gentle hands, spin you around, and smile.

She did all the special stuff that grammas do and children never forget. She colored. She sewed doll clothes. She let you play, suggested even, that you pull out the messy play dough at her kitchen counter. She took the kids to movies. The park. She played games. She got down on her knees on the floor. She had extraordinary one-on-one sleepovers at her house. She painted finger and toe nails. She played dress up and tea time. She baked cookies. She rode bikes and took walks. She colored Easter eggs. She sang songs. She created a palace for a playroom. She let you stand on the stool at the kitchen sink and help wash dishes. She always had popsicles in the freezer. She didn't care if you made a mess. She read books. She blew bubbles and took out sidewalk chalk on mild summer days. She rocked you to sleep. She gave hugs and kisses. She was affectionately called by all of the grandchildren, Gramma Jeannie. Excitement ensued when the kids were going to see Gramma Jeannie, and it is no wonder to us why. And now they miss her.

Wesley still goes running up the stairs every time he is at Mom and Dad's house. "Looking for Gramma Jeannie," he mumbles. He expects to see her in the spot he last remembered – on the hospital bed in the living room. We rush to scoop him up in our arms. We hold him tightly to us and tell him again that Gramma is in Heaven now. He scrunches up his face in momentary confusion, but then, it is as if he remembers Gramma is with Jesus and he is covered over with calm. Wesley touches us daily with his latest sign of affection. "Guess what?" we ask him. He responds in a long continuous one word phrase, "Iloveyoutoday!" His eyes sparkle and he giggles, knowing that we love to hear him say it. And we do.

Isaac is old enough to understand the magnitude of his Gramma Jeannie's absence. He talks about and misses the special moments with Gramma that are now memories. Alisha found him one night shortly after Mom died crying inconsolably in his bed. "I miss Gramma," he muttered as his chest heaved up and down between sobs. He is tender and reaches out to us. He even doesn't seem to mind or get embarrassed when Auntie Kayla kisses him on the cheek and won't let him say goodbye without telling her he loves her first. The children's innocent reflections of Mom are precious, and we are grateful that their memories are deep and wide. Gramma Jeannie is missed.

From: Pastor Michael Brandt <pastorbrandt@knowingthesavior.org>
To: Family and Friends in Christ
Subject: Jeannie Update 5/27/05

May 27, 2005,

Dear Family and Friends in Christ,

Jeannie's life verse, "Thy words were found and I ate them, and Thy words became for me a joy and the delight of my heart; for I have been called by Thy Name, O Lord God of Hosts," Jeremiah 15:16. She did (eat - receive His Word, He is the Word). They were (joy - her life's delight and meaning). She was (called by His Name - a child of God, by faith in Christ). She is (in His presence - with the Heavenly Host). Praise be to Thee, O Christ.

Jeannie's Celebration of Life Service was full of worship. The worship of her Creator and Redeemer brought comfort and strength to our hearts. The sanctuary and auditoriums were graced by loving family and friends. How beautiful the loving support of friends is, to a grieving soul. We are grateful for each one who could come and all who prayed from a far. We are especially grateful to our church staff and church family, as well as, the Sioux Falls Surgical Center family. Your sacrifices of love have embraced our hearts in ways we can never fully explain. How beautiful it was to see pews filled with care givers, honoring the memory of the 'care giver' God had entrusted to our family. Thank you.

Through Elden Nelson's lead and Scripture readings, our focus was drawn from the beginning to the God of everlasting life and the Conqueror of sin, death, and the devil. Her brother Jim's tribute was glorifying to God and eloquently honoring to a life well lived. The praise team, the accompanists, Jay's hymn leading, and Eric Dub's solo, all musically lifted us to say, "I'm Trusting You Alone". Rev. Lee's proclamation of Jeremiah 15:16 both nourished our souls and called us to personal commitment to Christ. It was a celebration with purpose and meaning!

Boy am I tired.

Now, don't panic. I'm not having an emotional meltdown. I haven't 'hit the wall'. A spiritual burnout isn't in the works. I'm not as some of you might say, "Finally, taking off the mask of being super Christian, pastor, husband, father, ...". I'm just tired.

I should be. God has taken Jeannie, me, our family, and many of you through quite a journey. From the dark depths of despair to exhilarating heights of glory, with countless up and downs inbetween, the Holy Spirit has exercised our faith. Wow, what a work out. I'm tired.

Each step of the way, He provided Heaven's oxygen of sustaining grace. However, once in a while, He would have to remind me to breathe. Remember, I'm Norske. There was a life to be lived. There was a valley of death to enter. There were fears to face and surprising joys to experience. Along the way decisions had to be made. Prayerful, heart-wrenching, finalizing decisions, which could not be avoided. Ones that needed to be diligently weighed and made in the counsel of God's Word. Hey, I'm tired.

In the midst of it all, it is wonderful to know that the presence of God and the sufficiency of His grace does not mean, we don't get tired. Remember Jesus rested, even in a storm tossed boat? Remember His sensitive words to His disciples, "Come away by yourselves to a lonely place (a good description of South Dakota) and REST a while." (Mark 6:31) I'm going to do that, but just for a while! I'm taking a little break, preaching on Sunday, May 29th (I must let the radio listeners know what's happening), going to a Memorial Day Remembrance on Monday (so should you), and then a little more rest. Then I'm back in the 'saddle again' (for you East Coasters, that are receiving these e-mails, this is a South Dakota-ism meaning work).

You see, there is a life I'm called to live. It will not be the same. It shouldn't be. It will have its 'moments'. But, it will be good, because God has ordained it to be so. God is good. His ways are beyond questioning (though He allows us to). His plans have a purposeful future and a sustaining hope. Jeremiah 29:11-14 tells me this ... in Him, I have a future and a hope ... I come in prayer, He listens ... I seek, He is revealed ... He is found, I am restored. Life's up and downs are real, but God is good and His grace is more than sufficient. I refuse to live any other way. I believe this is the choice all of us should make, every day ... no matter what!

Now, let me share an observation from the light, yet hopefully insightful side. Jeannie loved nature, but thought it should stay outside our house. A few years back I shot a good sized mule deer buck. Hey, I'm not bragging. It was big. Bigger than anything my gun toting brother-in-law or my boisterous, attorney nephew have ever shot. I had a shoulder mount made. After much prayer and whining, Jeannie let me hang it in our fireside room. Her words were, "Maybe for a year." That was 3 years ago. Well, on Thursday I went out to the cemetery to see if everything was in order. The dirt was mounded up for future settling and the family floral arrangement was place neatly on top. Everything looked proper. Then on closer review, I saw it. It was an imprint in the mound of dirt. It was the foot print of a deer, one who probably nibbled on our floral tribute. Yes, one beautiful deer print. On earth Jeannie could not get away from one DEAR hanging around and another deer hanging on a wall. Her earthly remains still can't, we're still 'hanging' around.

Fitting, I thought, as I honored the earthly remains of the DEAR I had passionately pursued all of my life, here was a representative print of a deer I pursue only for momentary pleasure. One has an everlasting value, the other only temporary. By the way, you who still have your DEAR with you, keep passionately pursuing her above all temporary pursuits.

* The following is for my girls. Girls, I'm too tired to check this for mistakes. When you find them, don't tire yourself out by thinking you have to tell me. My reputation won't suffer and neither will yours. In fact, most people marvel that I can turn on a computer.

Tired, But Resting For A While,
Michael

Chapter Twenty-four:
The Reality of Grief...

Kayla Brandt

Undoubtedly, nothing is quite the same. Life is very lonely without a mom. A wife. A grandma. But grief is an enigma. I don't know if one can know how to grieve, but you find yourself engulfed in sadness one moment and other times spilling over with joy. It takes a lifetime to heal. The initial days after Mom's death were confusing. We felt lost—in disbelief at the time that had just escaped us and the reality that we were now forced to face. It was like slamming into a brick wall no matter what way you turned. My car steered in the direction of Mom and Dad's house on auto pilot every day after work. But she wasn't there to take care of any more. I'd realize my mistake about halfway there and then drive around aimlessly for a time not knowing where to go or what to do next. We girls have all picked up the phone countless times to call Mom with news, a need, or nothing at all. You begin to dial. You realize. You hang up. You can't set foot in her house without remembering.

Dad had it the worst. Natural anticipation would build up in him on his drive home at the end of a long day. He'd looked forward to coming home to his wife of 36 years. But there would be no greeting at the door. No smile. No smell of dinner cooking. No ears to hear your voice. No voice to fill your ears. Just a dark house, quiet and empty now. Grief leaves you fumbling around for a while. You get angry. You get jealous. You get sad. And you learn to exercise more caution and care in all that you do. Yes, we miss Jeannie.

-- ✉ --

From: Pastor Michael Brandt <pastorbrandt@knowingthesavior.org>
To: Family and Friends in Christ
Subject: Jeannie Update 6/12/05

June 12, 2005,

Dear Family and Friends in Christ,

"When we asunder part, it gives us inward pain; but we shall still be joined in heart, and hope to meet again." (verse 4 of the hymn "Blest Be the Tie That Binds"

I'm lonely.

Again, I must remind you, "Don't panic!" I really am okay. God is great and His grace is sufficient. The Holy Spirit is comforting me and my family. He is giving each one of us strength to face each new day and every twist and turn of this journey. Yes, He is good. We must walk through this sorrow. There is no way around it. Jesus will carry us through. He is doing that right now.

"Turn to me and be gracious to me, for I am lonely and afflicted. The troubles of my heart are enlarged; bring me out of my distresses. Look upon my affliction and my trouble, and forgive all my sins," Psalm 25: 16-18. These precious verses were shared with me by Kayla (my third daughter). The one I've now written back into the estate! She wrote them on a note card and taped them to my bathroom mirror. What a treasure. What a comfort.

But, I'm lonely.

I should be. My girls and their families are lonely. In fact, if you knew Jeannie as a friend, you will have a certain loneliness too. It is only reasonable. Yes, it is right to be lonely. Not easy, but it is right. A person who loved you, and one you loved, is gone from this life. She is not missing. We do know where she is. The Bible tells us clearly that those who have surrendered to

Christ are taken immediately upon their death to be with Him in Paradise. Remember the thief on the cross? Just before his death, in the shame of his sin, he openly repented and Confessed his faith in Jesus, as King of Kings. Jesus said to him, "TODAY, you will be with me in Paradise."

It's a painful loneliness. When a person loses their mate, it should be painful. The death of any loved one is painful, but especially the loss of a life's mate.

Why? To answer this, we must consider the truths about marriage that are revealed in Scripture. First, marriage is a covenant. A covenant made between God and two people. A covenant made before God by two people to one another. Second, marriage is a miracle. God says, "The two shall become one!" Only God can do that. Then He says, "Let NO ONE put this union asunder." To do so is to mock God and vandalize His work. The oneness He has created is to be cherished and treasured. It is to be cared for and nurtured by daily commitment. Take time to read Ephesians 5:21-33.

Does that help you understand why the death of a mate is painful? It is like losing a limb. Part of you has been taken. Through death, the Great Physician has seen fit to amputate, remove, this precious part of you. Though we can not always fully understand why, it is a severing meant for His perfect will and purpose in our lives. He is not cruel. He is not removing a loved mate in careless disregard of your life. Rather, He is joyously receiving a loved one Home, while tenderly, by His Spirit, filling their absence here. But, it is painful. His Spirit comforts and heals.

However, I'm still lonely. It's extremely painful. The Spirit is comforting me. I am being healed. It will take time. God is loving. He is good. I love Him. I thank Him for giving me more than I deserve: my salvation, my marriage of 36 years, my four precious daughters, by three sons-in-law, my five grandchildren, my calling, my extended family, and friends like you. I'm also eternally grateful that He does not give me what my sinful self deserves. I would be eternally separated from Him.

The clothes in the closet, the fragrances of Jeannie, her decorating touch, her picky (she would say precise) organization are all precious reminders of the oneness I now miss. Some of you feel you're not doing enough to fill that void. As much as you would like to, you can not fill the loneliness. My girls can't. No one can. God alone can. He is. You can pray. Your love and kindness can be great encouragement. They are. It's going to be okay.

Walking Through the Sorrow with a Sure and Certain Hope,

Michael

Chapter Twenty-five: "A Little Bit..."

Kayla Brandt

B ut should we miss her? Again, it's the children who teach us. Isabelle skipped into Papa Mike's office at church one afternoon. Her blonde curls bounced on the top of her head and her voice bubbled with cheer.

"Hi, Grampa!" she shouted.

She searched the room for everything within arm's reach at 3-foot height, and her hands discovered their prize as she grasped onto a cross engraved with the name "Michael." She and Grandpa studied it together. Dad explained to Isabelle that the cross said his name and he attempted to help her sound it out. "Mmmm ... iiii," Dad began for her. Isabelle listened intently and as if experiencing a moment of epiphany exclaimed, "GRAMPA!" Dad couldn't squelch her delight. Close enough.

Out of the blue Isabelle glanced up at Dad and asked, "Do you miss Gramma?"

Isabelle's poignant question took Dad back for a moment before he replied, "Yes, I do. Do you?" he quizzed her back.

Isabelle stopped and pondered for a moment. She gazed up at Dad and raised her hand to show him her thumb and pointer finger spread about an inch apart, "Hmmm ... I miss Gramma a little bit."

And dear Isabelle is right. We should miss her just a little bit. We have to keep living. As hard as it is, little by little we settle into life again. And we should. We should be intent on pressing on with the work we have to do here on earth and toward the prize that awaits us in Heaven. When we set our hope on higher things, we shift from perpetual sadness to childlike joy that can miss Gramma *a little bit.*

From: Pastor Michael Brandt <pastorbrandt@knowingthesavior.org>
To: Family and Friends in Christ
Subject: Jeannie Update 6/27/05

June 27, 2005,

Dear Family and Friends in Christ,

I'm tired. However, He promised, "Come unto me, all you who are weary and heavy laden, and I will give you rest." I have come. He has given. I'm sleeping better. He is refreshing me in His Word and through your prayers on behalf of me and my family. Thank you.

I'm lonely. Yet, just as the Psalmist said, "The nearness of God is my good." Only He, Jeannie's Creator, could ever fill the void of her absence. He does. He says, "I will never leave you or forsake you." He doesn't. And once again, He is embracing us through the arms of His people.

I'm confident. Confident of Jeannie's well being. Confident of our well being. Confident, because He is acquainted, as the Scripture says, with every trial and hardship (Hebrews 4:15).

I'm content. Content with Him and His plan for my life. Content with His grace. Content by His grace.

How is this confidence and contentment possible? Am I just saying it, because it's the right thing to say? I'm a pastor, you know. Maybe, you think I'm just giving you the 'spiritually correct' line.

No, there is a reason, a living Reason. It's because of His love. He is love. His ways are loving.

His love causes me to gratefully rejoice over precious memories. It dries my tears. It restores my weary bones. It ignites hopes for today and for all eternity. It hears my faintest sigh and endures my loudest groanings. It dispels my darkest doubt and strengthens my flickering faith. It steadies my stumbling steps. It renews my vision and expands my dreams. It gently pushes me on, while tenderly preventing me from running. It is my stable foundation and my impenetrable covering. It fills me within and surrounds me without. God's servant Paul says it best in Roman 8: 37-39, "But in all these things we overwhelmingly conquer through Him who LOVED US! For I am convinced that neither death, nor life, nor angels, nor principalities, nor things present, nor things to come, nor powers, nor height, nor depth, nor any other created thing, shall be able to separate us from the love of God, which is in Christ Jesus our Lord."

Love makes me confident. It enables me to be content. Is He your confidence, your contentment? He wants to be. He wants to be 'the Love of your life'. Ask Him to be your all in all. When He is all you want, you will have all you need!

Talking about needs, some of you kind ladies have been concerned about my meal planning. Saturday before last, a lady called at 9 am and asked, "Pastor, have you had breakfast this morning?" I said, "Yes." But that answer wasn't enough for her. "What did you have?" "Coffee," I said. "That's not breakfast," she harped. "Well, I had something to eat too," I snapped (not my finest moment). She wouldn't give up, "What did you have?" "I had a man's perfect breakfast," I said, "Two pieces of cold pizza!" She ended our conversation with a disapproving sigh. Hey, it tasted good! I'm content.

Yesterday, I drove 40 miles for a pancake and a runny egg! How smart was that? But, anything to keep women happy and content!

Confident and Content in His Love,
Michael

Chapter Twenty-six: Still Crying Out To Jesus...

Kayla Brandt

It was the child in Isabelle who also bestowed transparency upon my grief. Three months after Mom's death our family had a moment to gather again. This time it was to celebrate. We were still adjusting to Mom's absence. We found comfort in holding fast to each other hard and often. We clung. This time of healing found us together at an annual Christian music festival, LifeLight. It was Labor Day weekend and we joined together every night to listen to the music and allow the comfort of the Holy Spirit to fill us up. We spread out our blankets and lawn chairs in the grassy field, devoured the fair food, and relished in the company of family and fellow believers surrounding us. It was an event that Mom had looked forward to and attended the past five years. She loved music. She loved to praise her King. Her voice was a spectacular choir all on its own.

I found my mind drifting back to the year before. Mom had literally dragged me along for the festivities. I was reluctant to go and found it easier to busy myself with mundane trivial tasks. I tried to exempt myself with complaints about the hassle of parking, time constraints, and hating large crowds, but Mom would hear nothing of my poor excuses. She knew that I needed to hear the truth. She also knew that if she tugged on my heart, I would not let her down. I couldn't disappoint my mom. I begrudgingly attended one night of the festival and ended up in awe of my mother. I watched as she stood and joined in the singing. She danced. She raised her hands in praise. She was uninhibited. Every ounce of her being was caught up in echoes of the truth resounding from the music. She was so alive. I was astonished by her joy. It was a place I hadn't reached in my faith, yet I was moved as I watched my mother dance at the throne of Jesus right here on earth.

This year, my heart desired to go to the festival. It was a gathering of believers. I belonged. As a family we sang and laughed together. During one song I scooped up Isabelle in my arms. The beat of the drums was loud, the rhythm swift and together they set our feet fancy and free. Isabelle squealed with delight as I spun her around and bounced her in my arms.

"Guess what?" she hollered at me. Her face was square across from mine with only about two inches separating us.

"What?" I shouted back.

"Gramma Jeannie goes to parties like this every day now!" she shrieked.

I gave a confirming nod, smiled, and we continued to dance. And she was right. What a party to look forward to.

Third Day performed the last night of the festival. Their message was clear as they recalled the process they went through to write the music for their latest album and how, upon completion, they discovered nearly every song told of the hope we have in Christ. The darkness of the night surrounded us and the crowd fell silent as Third Day began to sing their final song.

"To everyone who's lost someone they love, long before it was their time. You feel like the days you had were not enough when you said goodbye." Two lines. Our racing hearts stopped. Four sets of eyes sought contact with each other. Jeannie's girls were prepared to protect each other when the next lines came.

"And to all of the people with burdens and pains keeping you back from your life, you believe that there's nothing and no one who can make it right..." Our shoulders sank down with the weight of sadness. We instinctively reached for the hand of the sister next to us and grasped on. The chorus was coming next.

"Cry out to Jesus... Cry out to Jesus..."

Our tears began to pour in steady streams down our faces. We'd been holding our breath and now gasped in and out. The dark night brought the privacy needed to cry, and we were grateful. We wept.

We had heard Mom say the same four words to us, and now we heard them again. And we did cry out to Jesus in that still, sacred moment. Though immersed in grief, we were sheltered and covered with the comfort that only Jesus can bring. It was a time to grieve and a time to heal. It was a time for the weary to find rest. It was a time for the grace and mercy of Jesus to be sent and received by Jeannie's girls.

You'll find that grace and mercy, too.

It's been sent for you to receive.

But only if you cry out.

To Jesus.

From: Pastor Michael Brandt <pastorbrandt@knowingthesavior.org>
To: Family and Friends in Christ
Subject: Jeannie Update 9/1/05

August 1, 2005,

Dear Family and Friends in Christ,

"Blessed be the Lord, who DAILY bears our burden, the God who is our salvation. God is to us a God of deliverances; and to God the Lord belong escapes from death," Psalm 68: 19, 20

It is good for me to be able to write to you. Over the days of Jeannie's illness, we hoped our writing would be helpful to you. We wanted you to know what was happening and how we were doing. So I wrote. Then, when God graciously saw fit to take Jeannie unto Himself and in the days that have followed, I have needed, and have wanted, to stay in touch. I have selfishly hoped you would keep on praying for me and my family. We deeply believe that God hears and answers every prayer prayed in Jesus' Name. Thank you for being such faithful friends.

Someone said to me the other day, "Pastor, someday, sooner or later, things will return to normal." I knew what they meant, but I also knew that things can not return to what was 'normal.' Jeannie is gone, good for her! But what was normal for us will never be the same, normal again. We have to face this reality. Praise God we don't need to face it alone. Daily He bears our burdens. By His mercy and grace, He enables us to face the difficult moments and at the same time, rejoice in every great memory.

It may be difficult to deal with at times, but it is not bad. God had a 'NEW NORMAL' for me and my family. It will be good and great, for He is a good and a great God! It will come by His grace. It will come in His time. As hymn writer Carolina Berg wrote, "Day by day and with each passing moment, strength I find to meet my trials here. Trust in His wise bestowment, I have no cause to worry or to fear. He whose heart is kind beyond all measure gives unto each day what He deems best, lovingly its part of pain and pleasure, mingling toil with peace and rest." Yes, day by day, we are finding the NEW NORMAL of God's plan for the remainder of our lives. In fact, he ushered in a big new normal this past week. Well, not big in size, but in change. Early (12:30 am) Thursday, July 28th, Joseph Dale DeWitt, 7 lbs. 2 oz. and 19 in. long, was born to Erika and Sherwin. Praise God for His marvelous gift of life, a pleasant change with many 'changes' (literally) to come!

I have also realized that many, who need a NEW NORMAL are sadly satisfied with waht has been normal to them. They are satisfied with their normal 'goodness,' the 'normal' vices, their 'normal' religious habits, and all the while they are abnormal from God's point of view. The Bible tells us that God sees their vices as evil (remember Jesus' words to a religious man, Nicodemus, in John 3:19), and their religious activity as form only, void of the Spirit's power (2 Timothy 3:5). A NEW NORMAL is desperately needed. The Good News is this, Our Heavenly Father is in the business of making all things new, including people (2 Corinthians 5:17). If you haven't done so, ask Him to make you a new person in Jesus.

Creative cooking is a whole new issue too. Over a delicious, frozen pizza, Kayla gave me the bad news the other night. She said, "Dad, we have to go grocery shopping." Like that is going to do any good. She can't cook either, unless you call pouring milk on frosted mini wheats cooking. Then she said, "We'll have to take a cooking class." Is she crazy? Can you imagine me in a cooking class? Jeannie tried to help me when she was ill. It was a disaster. I'm still suffering from my attempts at domestic food prep skills. Back in late

April, I had used our outdoor grill. The salt was sticking in the shaker. Jeannie said, "Michael, put new salt in the shaker and add some rice to absorb the moisture." "Okay," I said. Well, the other day I used the grill again. I used the salt. Have you ever had crunchy salt on a hamburger? Jeannie never said what size of rice to use. Here's a 'Michael Grillin' Tip,' make sure the rice is bigger than the holes in the shaker.

Now, for the way I see it. Minerva's has a kitchen. They evidently go grocery shopping every week. They have somebody back there, maybe even more than one somebody, who has taken a cooking class and passed. Why should I duplicate their efforts? I'm just going to ask the council for a raise. Bon Appetit!

Day by Day, Following the God of Deliverance,
Michael

From: Pastor Michael Brandt <pastorbrandt@knowingthesavior.org>
To: Family and Friends in Christ
Subject: Jeannie Update 11/23/05

November 23, 2005,

Dear Family and Friends in Christ,

"But as for me, I trust in Thee, O Lord, I say, 'Thou art my God. My times are in Thy hand; ..." Psalm 31:14, 15a.

I knew I wanted to write to all of you, at least one more time. I just didn't know when it would be. Each time I would sit down to write, God would check my Spirit. Then a few days ago, the Words from Psalm 31:1-3 were impressed upon my heart. Like David, I am thankful to declare, "In Thee, O Lord, I have taken refuge; let me never be ashamed; in Thy righteousness deliver me. Incline Thine ear to me, rescue me quickly; be Thou to me a rock of strength, A stronghold to save me. For Thou art my rock and my fortress; for Thy Name's sake Thou wilt lead me and guide me."

When I was out to Jeannie's grave site in October, the dirt over her casket had finally settled. We knew it would. I weeded the ground and leveled it with fresh soil. Then, I planted some rye and a mixture of regular and dormant grass seeds. Now, we prayerfully hope it will take root. We want to present a cared for site. We have this same desire in our personal witness. The girls and I want you to see God's weeding and planting in our lives. He is caring for us. Many of you have faithfully been a part of His care force. Your prayers and words have been both sunshine and rain, causing our lives to grow in God's grace and comfort. Thank you for being faithful caregivers.

More than likely, next spring will bring more settling and a need for more soil and more seed. I'm sure there will be more settling in our adjustments too. Old and new sorrows, additional decisions, reoccurring emotional and spiritual needs can be expected. Just like now, our Heavenly Father will not abandon His plot, but faithfully come with the soil and seed of His loving-kindness and mercy.

I can't think of a better time than the Thanksgiving - Advent -Christmas Season to write, what will probably be my last Jeannie Update. Contrary to what you might think, I have more to be thankful for, than ever. I have more to look forward to, than ever. I have more reason to celebrate the real meaning of Christmas, than ever.

Though our family's life and many of your lives will sense a void because of Jeannie's passing, we all have reason to rejoice over the gift of her life. "Now Thank We All Our God With Hearts and Hands and Voices, Who Wondrous Things Has Done, In Whom This World Rejoices." It would be tragic, if the girls and I allowed the disappointment of unrealized dreams to steal our gratefulness for every moment we shared Jeannie's life as a loving wife, mother, grandmother, and friend. Her love, her voice, her touch, her listening ear, her fitting words, her gentle hands, her caring ways are missed, but even more so they are cherished through unceasing thanks to her Creator and Redeemer.

Advent wondrously reminds us that one day, sooner than we think, Jesus will come again. "O Come, O Come, Our Immanuel, and Ransom Captive Israel (Believers)."

What a reunion that will be. A forever, never to be separated again, perfect experience of eternal life! It reminds us to daily live for Christ. The days and sorrows pass more quickly, when you faithfully work and eagerly wait to see Jesus, face to face.

Christmas, too, reminds us that Jesus came to meet the sadness of death, head on, by conquering sin, satan, and the grave. "Joy To The World, The Savior Has Come" His coming was for the Brandts and for all who have lost loved ones. The matchless love of a God, who would send His Son to give His life, so we, who believe, would not perish, but have everlasting life. "Silent Night, Holy Night" remind us of the unspeakable joy of a radiant Savior's Star that shines in our darkest nights.

Yes, our times are in His hand. Our lives are surrendered to His will. Our future is held in His care. We will never be put to shame. These are the same truths, we hope you have come to embrace by faith in the one and only Son of God, Jesus Christ.

Unashamedly In His Hand,
Pastor Brandt

P.S. My desire in writing these Updates was two fold. First, I wanted you to know how and what we were doing. Second, I wanted to share the simple truths of Salvation by grace, through faith in Christ alone. If you desire to know more, go to our web-site <knowingthesavior.org>. Click on the link marked salvation. Let us know what Christ is doing for you and how we can be a continuing source of encouragement.

P.S.S. Some have suggested we bind these e-mails and use them as a tool to minister to others who are facing similar trials. A small group of people have been weighing the possibility of publishing them. If you have any comment, one way or the other, please let us know. By the way, if they are published, I want them to be 'as is', misspellings and all.

Epilogue

Dear Fellow Sojourners and Pilgrims,

"By faith Abraham lived as an alien in the land of promise, as in a foreign land dwelling in tents with Isaac and Jacob, fellow heirs of the same promise; for he was looking for the city which has foundations, whose architect and builder is God," Hebrews 11:9, 10.

It has been nearly a year since Jeannie ended her pilgrimage and entered into the Promised Land. From her new perspective of time, it has merely been the blink of an eye. The girls and I have done some blinking too. We have blinked away many tears these past several months. Each of us has celebrated a birthday, as well as, each of the major holidays. We have seen the date of Jeannie's birth and the date of our Anniversary come and go. Time has passed, countless blinks, but every tear has been noted by our Heavenly Father. In fact, Psalm 56:8 says, "Thou hast taken account of my sojourning; put my tears in Thy bottle; are they not in Thy book?"

Some days fly by, while other days seem to languish on. However, every day has been a day of grace. Like the manna in the wilderness, it has been just enough for the day. Enough for days of laughter and enough for days of tears ... always just enough. Our pilgrimage continues. Just like our Redeemer and our Heavenly Father, our Comforter and Guide is faithful and true. In days of 'tent dwelling in a foreign land', we walk on, grateful for fellow travel companions, heirs of the same promise. The encouragement and comfort we have received from these fellow pilgrims, cannot be measured. Its value is priceless. Its reward is eternal. Thank you for continuing to travel with us.

Along the way, some new pilgrims have been added to our family. One came by natural birth, his name is Joseph Dale DeWitt, son of Erika and Sherwin. He is a blessing. We will tell him about his Gramma Jeannie. By God's grace, he too will meet his Savior and his Gramma Jeannie one day. Other pilgrims have been added through the 'Second Birth'. Yes, even in our loss, Heaven made some gains. These new pilgrims had formerly been earthly citizens, bound by sin and death. Through Jeannie's suffering and death, God enabled them to face their own mortality. Witnessing the saving and sustaining grace of God in our lives, in desparation, they cried out to Jesus, "Save us." He heard and He did! The way I see it, you can never have too many pilgrims on this journey! This is one time the phrase, "The more, the merrier," really makes sense.

What's up ahead? More traveling, I expect. How much longer? Not too much longer, the signs along the way tell me we're getting closer. When Jeannie and I were traveling in the car, I would sometimes start to whistle or hum. Sadly, unlike her, I never knew the complete lyrics or tune to any song. So, I would get stuck on one phrase or measure, over and over. After a while, she'd subtly say, "Are we getting close, Michael?"

Well, I'm stuck again. Can you hear me? "I've got a mansion, just over the hill top ... I've got a mansion, just over the hill top ... I've got a mansion just over the hill top." Getting close, Michael? Yes, I believe it's just a hill or two away.

Onward and Upward, I'm Homeward Bound,
Michael, Jeannie Brandt's traveling companion

P.S. By the way, do you have a heavenly mansion? I know the Architect personally, if you haven't made an arrangement, He wants you to call on Him. "For whoever will call on the Name of the Lord (Jesus) will be saved," Romans 10:13